In this immensely practical book, Sa
both the "why" and the "how" of m
safe place for the most vulnerable in your care. *Make My
Church Safe* provides specific policies and procedures that
every church leader can implement—chapters 5 and 6
alone are worth the entire book! I hope every pastor and
seminary student will read this timely and crucial work.

KATIE J. McCOY, author of *To Be a Woman*


If there is anything a church should be, it's *safe*. However,
media reports of sexual abuse, financial misappropriation,
and failures of leadership are an everyday occurrence.
How can ministry leaders make sure that their church
doesn't make the nightly news? Sam Rainer gives readers
practical and timely advice for how to make sure their faith
community protects every person who enters their doors.

RYAN BURGE, associate professor of political science, Eastern
Illinois University


*Make My Church Safe* is a great and necessary resource
for church leaders. This book goes beyond protecting
churches from school shooters and sexual predators
to enable church leaders to understand the reality of
spiritual warfare, the inevitability of "Black Swan" events,
the importance of securing the church campus, and the
protection and equipping of children in a dangerous world.
Rainer also emphasizes that church safety is every member's
responsibility, and a Kingdom-first mindset. I highly
recommend this resource for churches and church leaders.

EDWARD E. MOODY, JR., executive director of the National
Association of Free Will Baptists

Make My Church Safe

# Make My Church Safe

*A Guide to the Best Practices to Protect Children &*
*Secure Your Congregation from Harm*

## SAM RAINER

TYNDALE
MOMENTUM®

*A Tyndale nonfiction imprint*

Visit Tyndale online at tyndale.com.

Visit Tyndale Momentum online at tyndalemomentum.com.

*Tyndale*, Tyndale's quill logo, *Tyndale Momentum*, and the Tyndale Momentum logo are registered trademarks of Tyndale House Ministries. Tyndale Momentum is a nonfiction imprint of Tyndale House Publishers, Carol Stream, Illinois.

*Make My Church Safe: A Guide to the Best Practices to Protect Children and Secure Your Congregation from Harm*

Designed by Ron C. Kaufmann and Claire M. Groppe.

All the examples and stories in this book are true. Names and some specific details have been modified to protect the privacy of the individuals involved.

Unless otherwise indicated, Scripture quotations are taken from the *Holy Bible*, New Living Translation, copyright © 1996, 2004, 2015 by Tyndale House Foundation. Used by permission of Tyndale House Publishers, Carol Stream, Illinois 60188. All rights reserved.

Scripture quotations marked NASB are taken from the (NASB®) New American Standard Bible,® copyright © 1960, 1971, 1977, 1995, 2020 by the Lockman Foundation. All rights reserved. www.lockman.org.

For information about special discounts for bulk purchases, please contact Tyndale House Publishers at csresponse@tyndale.com, or call 1-855-277-9400.

ISBN 978-1-4964-8840-4

Printed in the United States of America

| 30 | 29 | 28 | 27 | 26 | 25 | 24 |
|----|----|----|----|----|----|----|
| 7  | 6  | 5  | 4  | 3  | 2  | 1  |

*Dedicated to the survivors.*

*For justice—swift and complete.*

# Contents

# A DUAL CALLING

"They are not doing *anything*. The problem is being swept under the rug."

The director of a long-standing and successful church preschool ministry was calling for advice.

"This child is a potential danger to himself and to others around him."

She described a challenging situation—a preschooler who reacted violently in unpredictable ways. When he acted out, he was difficult to restrain. The teachers were concerned his behavior would continue to escalate and he might harm another child.

The preschool director had reported the behavior to the lead pastor multiple times. She wanted to create an intervention plan for the child and inform the right people about the problem. At their most recent meeting, she had pleaded with the pastor for permission to act. But he had reminded her in subtle ways that the child's grandfather was an elder in the church and a major financial contributor. The director was well aware of the grandfather's stature in the congregation. She was also aware of his reputation as a bully who used his wealth to leverage relationships in the church and the community.

"I'm stuck," she said. "At some point, this child will do something that will require us to make a report beyond our internal systems. Whether it's Child Protective Services or—"

"And people will blame you for not taking action earlier," I added.

"Exactly. I've been in this role for thirty years. I know how to deal with problematic children. I'm now caring for pre-schoolers whose parents were in my classes when I started."

She was right. She was knowledgeable, experienced, and cool under fire. The church and the community loved her. During her three decades of service, thousands of children had come through her program. The preschool ministry was one of the best parts of the church, and it was how many in the community knew the church was there. There was a long waiting list for admission, and family and friends packed the sanctuary for every preschool event.

But this situation was unlike anything she had ever encountered. The new pastor was playing favorites with certain elders, and the child's grandfather was part of a group attempting to rework the rules of church governance to give the elders more power and access to budget funds. The preschool director was not the only one affected by the changes, but her issues were particularly acute because children were involved.

"We have to prioritize safety," she said. "Yes, our reputation is at stake, but I'm most concerned about the children. This problem is solvable."

I watched as she folded her hands as if she were about to pray, but she looked straight ahead with fierce determination. "There are so many real dangers in the world," she continued. "We cannot invite them into our church."

Every church has a dual calling when it comes to the evils of the world: *ensure safety* and *confront danger*. The church must be a place where every person is protected from harm. The church is also called to send people out to preach the gospel in dangerous places. Churches are not islands in the community, set up to isolate believers from the ills of society. The walls of the church are not a protective barrier to keep out community problems. Instead, the church is a vehicle engineered by God to send people into the neighborhood and the wider world to confront the darkness and rescue lost sheep.

Internal safety creates a strong platform for people to become courageous gospel ambassadors. A safe church is a threat to the enemy of our souls. An unsafe church undermines the gospel and is thus an asset to the enemy.

The purpose of this book is to help train churches in this dual calling. Every church should be a safe space for everyone who comes in. Every church should also be equipping people to confront the powers of darkness and help those in trouble. Unfortunately, far too many churches are unsafe internally, while at the same time they're unwilling to confront external dangers. An unsafe church creates a toxic environment that works against the gospel. A safe church is battle-ready to combat the worst of the world's problems.

"I will do the right thing, even if it costs me personally," the preschool director told me. She was willing to sacrifice everything for the children and families she served. Like an experienced shepherd, she was ready to stand against any danger that came near her little ones.

## The Safety of the Shepherd

Too often, in our Sunday school stories of the Good Shepherd, Jesus is depicted as an *idyllic* figure—charming and simple, often watching his sheep in unspoiled and rustic settings. But the Good Shepherd isn't idyllic; he is a down-to-earth, down-in-the-dirt, lay-down-his-life-for-the-sheep *ideal* shepherd, willing to grapple with all dangers. He is the standard of perfection when it comes to caring for his flock.

Sheep are mentioned more than any other type of livestock in the Bible, and the occupation of a shepherd is a common one in biblical stories. Abel, Moses, David, and Amos were all shepherds, and shepherds were some of the first people to see Jesus after his birth.[1] God's people are often described as sheep. In Genesis 48:15 and Psalm 23:1, God himself is described as a shepherd, and Micah portrays the coming Messiah as a shepherd.[2] In the Gospels, Jesus says of himself, "I am the good shepherd; I know my own sheep, and they know me."[3]

Shepherds in the first century were common, but of low standing. They slept beside their sheep and kept constant watch over them. Not surprisingly, shepherds smelled like sheep. Caring for sheep meant rescuing them from all sorts of predicaments. For the most part, sheep are slow and defenseless. They need a shepherd. We, too, like sheep, need an outside source of protection. Whether we realize it or not, we are entirely dependent on God.

Sheep are not only defenseless, but they are also valuable. Their wool, skins, and meat were all important commodities in the agrarian culture of Jesus' day. Sheep were a common target for thieves because they were worth the effort to steal. This truth is also at the heart of the gospel.

> I am the gate. Those who come in through me will be saved. They will come and go freely and will find good pastures. The thief's purpose is to steal and kill and destroy. My purpose is to give them a rich and satisfying life.
>
> I am the good shepherd. The good shepherd sacrifices his life for the sheep.
>
> JOHN 10:9-11

> My sheep listen to my voice; I know them, and they follow me. I give them eternal life, and they will never perish. No one can snatch them away from me, for my Father has given them to me, and he is more powerful than anyone else. No one can snatch them from the Father's hand.
>
> JOHN 10:27-29

The Good Shepherd is always "close beside" you (Psalm 23:4). Whatever you experience, God experiences it with you. He is always there, through bad weather and danger from wild animals. When one sheep is lost, Jesus is quick to pursue it. Even one wayward sheep makes the flock incomplete.

Our safety in the Good Shepherd is rooted in his transcending power and glory. Life with the Good Shepherd is comforting, not because he fulfills our desires, but because we find our purpose in fulfilling his desires. We should not "look out for number one,"[4] but instead look to the one in whom our "real life is hidden." Self-centeredness, self-promotion, and self-aggrandizement create a culture in which the most vulnerable are overlooked and even abused. We will always fail when we live for ourselves. But if we center our lives on serving and pleasing God, he will never fail us.

The key to understanding the safety found in the Good Shepherd is recognizing the connection between Psalm 22 and Psalm 23. The benefits of Psalm 23 do not happen without the sacrifice of Psalm 22. There is no "You are close beside me" in Psalm 23:4 without the "They have pierced my hands and feet" of Psalm 22:16. There are no "green meadows" in Psalm 23:2 without the "My God, why have you abandoned me?" of Psalm 22:1. Jesus is the sacrificial lamb of Psalm 22; and through his sacrifice he becomes the Good Shepherd of Psalm 23. The Suffering Servant becomes the Caring Shepherd.

## The Danger of the Mission

The turning point for me in thinking about church safety occurred at a funeral I officiated for a local family I didn't know. They had contacted our church asking for help with the service.

At one point, I was holding the four-year-old boy whose mother had passed away from an overdose of fentanyl and cocaine. I'll never forget what he said to me.

"Are you going to help bring my mommy back?"

I didn't have any words for him. Only tears.

As a consequence of his mother's death, the boy was placed in a foster home. Thankfully, it was one full of love and support. At about the same time as the funeral, a local newspaper headline caught my attention: "Bradenton Is Opioid Overdose Capital of Florida. And Still No One Knows Why."[5]

Every year, hundreds of children are removed from their homes in the county where I live. More than half of these situations are directly attributable to substance abuse by their parents or guardians. Most of the children removed are under the age of five. I didn't have the words to reassure that four-year-old boy, but his question prompted me to act. I couldn't bring his mom back, but my wife and I could become foster parents for children in situations like his. So we got our license and began our foster journey.

The foster system in our area is stretched thin. When willing families become licensed, they receive a child placement immediately. My wife and I recently cared for an infant experiencing the effects of cocaine exposure. When addictive drugs a pregnant mother consumes are passed from her bloodstream through the placenta, her baby may be born dependent on them. Withdrawal can be an awful experience as the tiny child's central nervous system tries to recover.

The Good Shepherd guided my wife and me into a system full of horrors so we could help children find green meadows and peaceful streams.[6] Our home is a safe space. Your church should also be a safe space. But that won't happen unless you take positive action to make it and keep it safe. The world is full of danger, and the church is called to the front lines.

Doing what's right often comes with a level of risk. We see the risk and reward of caring for a child in need in the story of Moses. When Pharaoh's daughter opened a basket that she found floating along the banks of the Nile, she saw a baby and said, "This must be one of the Hebrew children"[7]— that is, one of the children that her father, the pharaoh, was determined to kill.[8]

Imagine the desperation of Moses' mother, placing her baby in the papyrus basket and letting him drift away from the safety of her arms.

Imagine the courage of Moses' sister, Miriam. At significant risk to her own safety, she kept watching over the basket. When Moses was found, she became an advocate for him. She stayed close to the crisis to help. She risked everything when she reached out to Pharaoh's daughter.

Imagine the audacity of Pharaoh's daughter. She knew

her father had decreed that all Hebrew baby boys were to be killed, but she exercised her power as a member of the royal family and used her position to do what was right. The child in the basket moved her. A child in need should move all of us to action.

All the women in this story took tremendous risks, but fear didn't stop them from doing the right thing. What if every church were to view the foster care system in their area as a floating papyrus basket? What if, when the people of the church opened the baskets, they had the same response as Pharaoh's daughter? What if more of God's people were willing to take risks to help others in danger? Your church should be a haven of hope for people in need. I fear that our modern version of the Christian calling is too safe. At the same time, I'm concerned that our churches are not safe enough.

## The Spiritual Battle for Church Safety

Spiritual warfare is the basis for all conflict in the physical world—every geopolitical conflict, every argument with your spouse or kids, and every bit of melodrama on daytime talk shows. God doesn't want us to be at odds with each other, but Satan loves to distract the world and the church with hostility. Satan's fall from heaven happened because he believed he could be more powerful as God's *enemy* than as his *friend*. Remember, Satan is intelligent but unwise. He is strategic but flawed. He is powerful but defeated. Consider Peter's words of warning in his first letter.

Stay alert! Watch out for your great enemy, the devil. He prowls around like a roaring lion, looking for someone to devour. Stand firm against him, and be strong in your faith. Remember that your family of believers all over the world is going through the same kind of suffering you are.

1 PETER 5:8-9

How will Satan attempt to destroy you and your church? The father of lies wants you to be more focused on yourself than on him or God. Satan is fierce, relentless, ruthless, and shrewd. We must be alert and always on guard. Satan is not only against God, but he is also against you. He wants you distracted, detached, or dead. Distracted believers pursue their own goals apart from God. Detached believers are wayward or even absent from the body of Christ. And Satan would love for you to remain dead in your sins.

In Luke 11, when Jesus amazes everyone by driving out a demon, the people openly wonder about the source of Jesus' power. Some claim he must have struck a deal with Satan. Jesus reminds them that a house divided against itself cannot stand.

"But if I am casting out demons by the power of God," he says, "then the Kingdom of God has arrived among you."[9]

Then Jesus throws down the gauntlet, saying, "Anyone who isn't with me opposes me, and anyone who isn't working with me is actually working against me."[10]

Satan wants to destroy you. God wants to save you. The

church should be on the side of salvation and oppose all of Satan's destructive efforts. Satan was defeated the moment he refused to give God glory. As Jesus told his followers, "I saw Satan fall from heaven like lightning! Look, I have given you authority over all the power of the enemy."[11]

What did Satan look like in Genesis 3? A snake. He uses various physical forms to accomplish his spiritual warfare. Why? If we don't know what he looks like, we won't know when we encounter him. Satan wants you to think of him as a creepy creature in a horror film or like the cartoon figure with a pitchfork and horns. Horror makes us cower. Cartoons cause us to drop our guard. But these images are not what Satan actually looks like. While we are looking for horns and a pitchfork, he's showing us a mirror. Satan loves to deceive us by showing us something we like to see; namely, *ourselves*. The powers of darkness are quite adept at leading us astray. They've been doing this since the beginning of time. We are not their first assignment.

But Jesus, speaking of Satan, says, "He has no power over me."[12] So, don't live in fear. Don't be deceived. Live for Christ, and his truth will give you his courage and his power.

## Your Role in Church Safety

In writing this book, I hope to give churches a resource to equip their leaders and members for the dual calling of ensuring safety and confronting danger. When we hear the term *church safety*, we often think of active shooters and sexual predators. These two dangers are real, but they are only part of the threat. We will take a more comprehensive view of church safety here—though the book is designed to be brief and practical, so any church member can use it. I consulted several specialty experts while writing, but I do not intend for the book to be the end-all resource for each area of church safety.

The dual calling of ensuring safety and confronting danger means you have a dual responsibility. Your church should be a safe space for people seeking rescue or refuge. Additionally, your church should be willing to combat the spiritual forces of evil that affect every community. In nine concise chapters, we will discuss how to make the church a place of safety while also being dangerous to the forces of darkness.

Chapter 1 deals with the reality of spiritual warfare. If your church is pursuing God's mission in the world, you should expect opposition from the powers of darkness. Every obedient believer is a threat to evil, and you must be ready for Satan's schemes.

Chapter 2 examines the inevitable risks of ministry and how to mitigate the dangers. Because ministry involves *people*, some sort of incident will likely happen at some point in almost every church. Even "Black Swan" events—such as a pandemic or a natural disaster—require basic preparation plans.

Chapter 3 explores the systemic problems of sexual, physical, and emotional abuse. One of the most dreadful aspects of ministry is how to deal with instances of abuse. Every church needs a clear response pathway and a clear understanding of how to reduce the potential for harmful behavior.

Chapter 4 discusses how to secure a physical campus. This includes the basics of lockdowns, medical emergencies, active shooter planning, crisis prevention, and incident response. Safety procedures in a manual are useless unless everyone knows what they are and how to act on them.

Chapter 5 unpacks the best practices for protecting children from harm and equipping them for safety. This discussion will help children's ministry leaders protect and equip the children under their care.

Chapter 6 extends the discussion from the previous chapter to cover how churches can protect and equip students in ways that are age appropriate.

Chapter 7 will help you navigate the aftermath of a moral failure by a church leader. Church safety must include a healing process and an understanding of why the failure occurred. I hope your church never has to experience this pain, but some will, and all churches must be prepared.

Chapter 8 establishes how church safety is each individual church member's responsibility. Church safety won't happen unless every member commits to it. Everyone is responsible for reporting concerns. Don't let a lack of commitment to safety be the gap Satan uses to attack your church.

Chapter 9 points to the Kingdom strength of a safe church. When the church body is unsafe, it is unfit for battle. Safety first is a Kingdom-first mindset. Once a church is made safe internally, the people will be better equipped to put on the full armor of God to do battle against the powers of darkness.[13] Your church will not be effective in the Kingdom of God unless it is safe for the most vulnerable.

Satan's only real power in this battle is the power we give him. His power is based on our consent and compliance. He cannot overpower Jesus, so he focuses instead on trying to trick, trip up, and torpedo God's people. Do not fall for Satan's deception. Stand with Christ and create a safe church that is dangerous to the powers of darkness.

# THE REALITY OF THIS DARK WORLD

I remember pulling a book titled *This Present Darkness*, by Frank Peretti, off my dad's shelf when I was in third grade. I have no idea why he let me read it. The cover depicted giant bird claws in the sky creeping down like a hovering cloud over a small church. I could tell the novel was going to be scary, but my curiosity compelled me to read it.

Sales of *This Present Darkness* started off slowly, but the book soon became a cultural phenomenon as word of mouth spread about what is often considered the first popular work of Christian horror.[1] The inspiration for the title comes from Ephesians 6:12,[2] a verse in a section of Scripture cautioning believers against trying to battle the spiritual forces of darkness without God's armor. As the first adult fiction I ever read, it had a tremendous impact on me. Though a work of fiction, it made me realize that the dark world of evil spirits is real.

It might seem odd to start a discussion of church safety by talking about spiritual warfare. Unfortunately, the critical connection between the two is often missed, to the great detriment of our churches. No church will ever be safe if the leaders and members overlook, downplay, or dismiss the reality of spiritual warfare in our day-to-day lives.

We can do our best to live upright lives, and that might even be true of most Christians. But if we ignore the fact that we have a real enemy, the devil, who is constantly trying to drive a wedge between us and our Savior; that he "prowls around like a roaring lion, looking for someone to devour";[3] and that, like a real-life lion on the savanna, he's targeting the weak, the wounded, and the vulnerable, we will not be prepared to make our churches both safe to those who seek refuge there and dangerous to the workers of darkness.

Darkness simultaneously repulses and allures us. This dual effect is why we cover our eyes at horror movies but still get a thrill. It's why my eldest daughter loves the Haunted Mansion ride at Disney. It's why people both pursue and fear paranormal activity. The problem is that it's difficult to shut the door to the world of demons once you've opened it. How do you know where to draw the line? Perhaps one telltale sign is a feeling of spiritual oppression. Growing up, I watched every episode of *The X-Files*. The show was entertaining, but I never thought aliens might abduct me. However, the same show really spooked my wife when she was younger.

I recognize the nuances of these issues. Though I was allowed to read *This Present Darkness*, my parents would have grounded me for years if I had played with a Ouija board. Should Christians watch horror movies? Or read zombie apocalypse books? Should children take the Haunted Mansion ride while visiting the Magic Kingdom? Though questions like these may be important, focusing too much on them can cause us to overlook the bigger issues of spiritual warfare.

Satan will disguise himself as an angel of light.[4] He loves to be a false beacon of hope, drawing people closer through deception before they realize the dangers of the waters around them. The apostle John, in his first letter, advises the church to "test the spirits to see whether they are from God."[5] Here, John contrasts the Spirit of truth with the spirit of deception.[6] The problem is that counterfeit truth is often attractive. John warns the church of many false prophets who were denying the truth of Jesus. The early church did not have the full text of the Bible that we have today. Teaching was mainly oral, and house churches were spread out and often isolated. These churches relied on emissaries, or special messengers, to pass along doctrinal teaching. Paul sent Timothy and Silas. John sent elders. But sometimes, false emissaries arrived, claiming an authority that was not theirs. Some churches received false letters.

What happens when false teaching enters the church? Bad doctrine makes false promises that do not deliver. Bad doctrine devalues true teaching. Bad doctrine causes people to stop seeking God's will. Why is counterfeit truth so readily accepted? Because it's easy! It makes us feel good in the moment but leaves us without discernment in the long run. Not every sign or wonder is from God. Deuteronomy 13 warns of false signs and false miracles.[7] If supernatural activity doesn't point to God, it is meant to deceive us. If a sign or wonder doesn't cause us to marvel at the character and nature of God, then it is leading us astray. Consuming counterfeit truth is tantamount to cheating on a test in school, except the stakes are much higher. An exam is coming. Christ will return in judgment. The final is comprehensive, and there is no way we can pass if we've cheated our way through life with counterfeit truth.

## The Dangerous but Limited Power of Darkness

The spiritual battle between good and evil is more than an academic, metaphysical exercise. The unseen realm has daily practical implications in the seen world. During a revival in Ephesus under the apostle Paul, people burned books of sorcery with an estimated value of millions of dollars.[8] The people knew the impact of these books on their lives. As the late Warren Wiersbe famously noted, "The Christian life is not a playground; it is a battleground, and we must be on our guard at all times."[9] Our church activities are not like school recess, a respite from the long workweek. The local church is on the front lines of ministry. Though there is no beauty in warfare (spiritual or otherwise), the battling bride of Christ is a magnificent sight to behold. Despite the muck of this world, she remains pure and righteous. She belongs to Christ. She battles on behalf of Christ. She never stops engaging in the mission of reclaiming the captives of darkness. The beautiful bride is a tenacious, battling warrior.

In this battle, we must remember that the darkness is *hostile* but also *limited in power*. Adam and Eve sinned in the Garden of Eden because they fell into Satan's trap of deceit. All three parties faced the consequences of this sin. God told Eve that giving birth to children would come through painful labor. He told Adam that the pleasure of work would become painful labor. And when God addressed Satan, he placed him under a curse: "I will cause hostility between you and the woman, and between your offspring and her offspring. He will strike your head, and you will strike his heel."[10]

Our battle with evil began in the Garden. Ever since, there has been hostility between humanity and Satan. When God banished Adam and Eve from Eden, this hostility moved out into the world, where Satan's army of darkness has continued to fight throughout every successive generation.

Genesis 3:15, where God declares hostility between us and Satan, is also the first reference to Jesus in the Bible. There we learn that Satan has been defeated from the very beginning of human history. The stricken heel refers to the wounds Jesus received on the cross. But with that same heel, Jesus gave Satan a fatal blow to the head. In the course of time, through the offspring of Eve, our Savior would emerge on the world scene. God would enter the story of humanity through the incarnation of Christ and ensure the final victory.

Some might be surprised at the violence in the Old Testament. I'm not. Satan knew the prophecies about Jesus, but he didn't know precisely how God would come to earth—or when. So Satan sought to destroy anyone who could potentially be the Savior. In the New Testament, when Jesus the Messiah emerged, Satan worked hard to lure him away from his calling. After Jesus was baptized, he was led by the Holy Spirit into the wilderness, where Satan tempted him in every way. Satan will do everything he can to try to stop the Good News.

It is important to remember that Satan fights from a place of defeat. His attacks can hurt us, but his power is limited. Have you ever wondered why Satan doesn't just use raw power to destroy the church? He can't! If Satan could overpower the body of Christ, he would. Why is Satan limited in power? Because sin decreases strength. This is why Satan relies on deceit and not brute strength. The forces of darkness are real, but they are "securely chained in prisons of darkness."[11] The powers of darkness are no match for the powers of light. That's why Satan relies on lies.

Light always overpowers darkness. Jesus has absolute authority over Satan. Jesus gave this authority over demons to the disciples and the early church, and we have this same authority today. We can come under spiritual attack. Make no mistake, these attacks can hurt us. But demons and the spiritual forces of evil cannot overcome the church.

Satan has known from the beginning that he is defeated. Yet he fights on. When Jesus was born in Bethlehem, Satan tried to kill him through Herod's horrific plan to murder baby boys. Warned by an angel of the Lord, Mary and Joseph fled to Egypt, and God's sovereign plan continued to unfold.[12] When Satan couldn't kill Jesus, he tried to corrupt him with temptation. But Jesus prevailed.[13] Then, through the words of Peter, one of Jesus' closest friends, Satan tried to convince Jesus that the cross wasn't necessary.[14] Finally, Satan realized he couldn't prevent the cross, so he relished in it as much as he could. If Jesus was going to experience pain, then it might as well be excruciating pain.

Now that the plan of redemption is complete and Jesus has been revealed as the Messiah, Satan wants to keep people away from knowing how to be saved. He thinks if he can deceive people or hinder the spread of the Good News, maybe he can derail the plan.

Why does Satan keep fighting? Why not just give in, cut a deal, or repent? He is such a master of deceit that he has wholly deceived himself. If you've ever tried to help someone who is self-deceived, you know it is virtually impossible to get through to that person. Satan is as deep into deceit as one can go. He has only one goal: to deceive the world. He is hostile, but he is ultimately weak.

## The Power We Give Satan

Satan is absorbed in self-deception, and he wants to drag us down too. Every sin is ultimately rooted in the belief that we know better than God does. Satan is the father of lies, but where did he come from, and how can he be so completely deceived, even about himself? Satan began as Lucifer, the "shining star" and "son of the morning" mentioned in Isaiah 14:12. Lucifer did not produce light—he could only reflect the light of God—but he was so self-deceived that he believed he could be like God.

The prophet Ezekiel writes that Satan was a "mighty angelic guardian" in heaven prior to his fall.[15] Possibly, he was the leader of worship among the angels, but he tried to divert worship to himself. Like a dishonest broker, he was skimming praise from God.

How long was Satan the worship leader before God began creating the heavens and the earth? We don't know. Millions of years? Perhaps the creation of Adam and Eve caused Satan to become jealous. All we know for sure is that pride took him down.

Apparently he was something to behold. Ezekiel writes, "Your heart was filled with pride because of all your beauty."[16] How powerful is pride? Consider this: Satan was a *righteous creature* living in a *perfect realm,* and yet pride caused him to fall.

Unlike God, Satan cannot be in all places at once. Thus, he cannot be in all things at all times. But though he isn't omnipresent, he has many subordinates at his beck and call. So even though Satan isn't attacking us directly, his army of darkness is equipped and conscripted to tempt and deceive us on his behalf. Remember, our battle is not against flesh and blood. The demons want us focused on the physical world, because it gives them the upper hand when we're not engaged in the spiritual realm. The only real power Satan has is the power we give him. His power is based on our consent. He can't overpower Jesus, so he tries to trick you and me. Don't fall for his schemes. Stand firm, clad in the full armor of God.[17]

## The Power God Gives Us

"I will turn out the lights on the third floor," my wife said as we locked up the church following Wednesday night activities.

After finishing on the first floor, I waited for Erin to arrive—which took longer than I expected. Finally, the elevator bell sounded, and as Erin stepped through the doors and into the moonlight, I saw her bloodied face.

"What *happened*?" I said as I ran to her.

She was crying, or so I thought. No, she was laughing.

"You need to tell me what's going on," I said.

"I was creeped out by the dark and started running. But I misjudged the location of the elevator door."

She had run full force into a plaster wall and had broken her nose.[18]

How do our minds play such tricks on us? Why does a dark church building feel creepy on a rainy night? Of all places in the world, a church campus should feel secure. What controls our minds controls everything else. But God gives us the power to protect our minds. Ephesians 6:17 reveals that the helmet of salvation is part of our spiritual armor.

We should all be aware that Satan cannot read our minds. He doesn't know *what* we're thinking, but through his deceptive arts he can influence *how* we're thinking.

The spiritual battle for church safety begins in the minds of the congregation. If you don't *think* you can do anything, you won't take action. Satan can't take away your salvation, but he will try to keep your salvation from working for you. What should you do when you're facing a spiritual attack? How can you prepare your mind?

First, don't be afraid. "Fear not" is one of the most common commands in the Bible. You have the power of Christ in you. God is a God of peace, not disorder and chaos.

Second, pray out loud. Demons can't read your mind, but they can hear what you say and they are expert observers. Your prayers don't have to sound like elaborate ritualistic incantations. There's no need to be dramatic—just talk to God. That's what Jesus did. He simply talked to his Father.

Third, use the opportunity to repent of your sins. The power to resist demons comes from the Holy Spirit. During an attack is an excellent time to realign your will with God's.

Repentance can be a big part of that—whether or not your sin has opened a door to the enemy.

Finally, don't focus on the powers of darkness; focus on the truths of Scripture and the power of almighty God. God's power is released through his truth. God's truth is a fixed, objective standard by which all reality is measured. It is not based on our feelings or opinions. Relativism might be popular—until a personal crisis hits. Nobody wants their brain surgeon, for example, to operate based on the shifting standards of relativism. Nobody wants to hear, "Well, when I start the procedure, I'll open your skull and start digging around and see how I feel." No, when facing a serious concern, we want objective standards and absolute truth.

Church safety is certainly a serious concern, and we must approach it on the basis of God's truth—starting with the truth about God himself. If God is the giver of life, then Satan, in his opposition to God, is all about death. If God's Word is true, then Satan's word can only be false—and, therefore, whatever is false leads to death. If God is love, then Satan epitomizes hatred. Thus, all false truths and half-truths are born out of hatred.

Why do some believers fall prey to the mistruths of bad theology? The apostle Peter encourages those who are young in their faith to "crave pure spiritual milk so that you will grow into a full experience of salvation. Cry out for this nourishment, now that you have had a taste of the Lord's kindness."[19] The writer to the Hebrews concurs with this advice but warns about remaining too long as a spiritual newborn:

> You have been believers so long now that you ought to be teaching others. Instead, you need someone to teach you again the basic things about God's word. You are like babies who need milk and cannot eat solid food. For someone who lives on milk is still an infant and doesn't know how to do what is right. Solid food is for those who are mature, who through training have the skill to recognize the difference between right and wrong.
>
> So let us stop going over the basic teachings about Christ again and again. Let us go on instead and become mature in our understanding. Surely we don't need to start again with the fundamental importance of repenting from evil deeds and placing our faith in God. . . . God willing, we will move forward to further understanding.[20]

Accepting Christ does not make us mature believers. Accepting Christ makes us spiritual infants. No one should remain in spiritual infancy, never realizing or achieving their purpose. They remain dependent in all the wrong ways and can drag others down with their dependency.

Spiritual growth is critically important. We must learn how to tell the difference between good and bad theology, between a caring shepherd and a charismatic wolf. Truth is ultimately found in the person of Jesus Christ. To know the truth means that we know the one who is true. Knowing the truth about God hinges upon a right relationship with Jesus, who is divine truth. Jesus is the very truth of God!

The following chapters will demonstrate proactive ways the church can defeat evil by creating safe environments for discipleship. Darkness cannot hold back the movement of light. We're part of a movement that Jesus started, and hell cannot thwart it.

# MITIGATING THE RISKS OF MINISTRY

"We have not had a single incident in my twenty years here."

As an experienced church consultant, I was surprised by the man's comment. We were in conversation because the church needed help finding a new pastor and he was on the search committee. Over several minutes, we covered some basic topics, but he quickly became defensive when I inquired about church safety. Curious, I pushed the issue further.

"You've never reported anything to the authorities?"

"No, because nothing has happened."

"What about minor incidents, like a child biting another child?"

"Nothing like that. Ever."

I didn't think he was lying, but he was dangerously naive. Every church will have some type of safety issue, simply because ministry involves people. I was concerned that this search committee member was willfully ignoring the obvious. As we finished our call, I couldn't help wondering what had gone unnoticed and unreported in his church. How a church responds to the inevitable risks of ministry speaks volumes about whether the congregation places the lives of individuals over the reputation of the institution.[1]

In the introduction, I proposed the idea that every church has a dual calling: ensuring safety and confronting danger. This dual calling means that church leaders have a dual responsibility: creating a safe shelter for those in need of rescue, and preparing and sending out spiritual warriors to fight battles with evil. Churches that are safe on the inside are a threat to the presence of danger and evil on the outside. This chapter covers the main ways that churches can mitigate *internal* risks.

No church is risk-free. You cannot promise that nothing bad will ever happen. For example, my executive pastor recently came to me with a medium-sized bolt in his hand. It was sheared in half.

"What happened?" I asked.

"One of the canopies on the playground gave out and collapsed on the picnic table. But no one was there when it happened."

"How did that happen?"

"The company that installed the equipment used the wrong hardware."

He was already working on a solution to ensure that the playground equipment would be properly secured going forward.

Our playground hosts daily activities. The preschool uses it during the week, and it's popular on Sundays as well. The playground had gone through proper inspections, but the risk was undetectable. In this instance, our church had done everything we could to reduce risk, but we couldn't eliminate it entirely. But even though it's impossible to completely remove *all* risk from your ministry, it is important for every church to have training and systems in place to mitigate *known* risks.

What image comes to mind with the term *risk management*? Pocket protectors, spreadsheets, and algorithms? That's where my thoughts go. Perhaps the subject seems bland or academic, but proper risk management is a proactive way to identify, analyze, reduce, and evaluate potential hazards within your ministry.

> *Identify:* What might reasonably happen without intervention?
>
> *Analyze:* How likely is this risk? What is the potential impact of the risk?
>
> *Reduce:* What can reasonably be done to mitigate this risk proactively?
>
> *Evaluate:* Did the risk management policy work as designed?

Insurance company requirements and fear of lawsuits drive a lot of risk management policies in churches today. For example, requiring two teachers per classroom is a common practice in children's ministry. Additionally, not everyone in your congregation should be allowed to drive the church van, and your insurance carrier likely has some guidelines about who can drive and when. In the following chapters, we will go into greater detail about best practices in specific ministry areas, but for now, I want to emphasize the proper motivation for making your church safe. It isn't fear of litigation, but rather a desire to provide a safe and caring environment in which your ministry can thrive. Risk management is most successful in churches when driven by a theological conviction of caring leadership.[2] In short, our motivation should be less about reactive compliance and more about proactive shepherding.

Before I was a pastor, I began my professional career trading energy futures in the financial services industry. The Enron scandal had occurred the previous year, and many energy experts were reconsidering their corporate careers.[3] There were job openings that not many people wanted. At twenty-three years of age, I jumped into one of the most challenging markets in the world: California electricity futures. We had an entire group dedicated to risk management. Nothing happened at the company until the risk management team gave their assessment. The volatility of the commodity markets made it too risky to make large bets one way or the other. Our clients depended on us to mitigate the risk of their energy consumption.

Without proper risk management, our company would not have lasted more than a few months. If companies in turbulent markets prioritize risk management, how much more should churches look for ways to be as safe as possible?

## True Accountability for Safe Shepherds

Safe shepherds are accountable shepherds. The two cannot be separated. Safety and accountability go hand in hand. So what do safety and accountability look like for pastors, other key church leaders, and paid staff?[4]

Accountability is the acceptance of responsibility for one's actions. Accountability is more than having correct theology. For example, a church leader may believe in the biblical nature of accountability but not follow through—like a person who believes exercise is good for the body but never goes to the gym.

Accountability is more than having the right systems in place. Church leaders may submit to a system of accountability but do so grudgingly. Additionally, no system is perfect. Loopholes always exist. People who want to game the system will find ways to get around the rules.

Ultimately, true accountability is a spiritual discipline. Spiritual leaders should *seek* accountability as a vital component of spiritual maturity. Willing, proactive accountability is a spiritual discipline in which beliefs are put into action.

Accountability can be both formal and informal. In any work environment, including the church, expectations for proper behavior must be well established, well communicated, and well understood. These formal guidelines should be consistent, ethical, and reasonable.

In a church, accountability also occurs informally through the relational side of discipleship.

Consider the nature of accountability through three different layers: *culture, operations,* and *personal integrity.*

Whenever a group of people share a system of values, beliefs, and behaviors, they create a culture. Though there are many informal ways to build culture, a written covenant formalizes the church's expectations of its members. Many churches have membership covenants, but an additional covenant between pastors and their churches is also helpful. A clearly written covenant means there is less chance for unmet expectations to cause conflict.[5]

Church operations include the day-to-day activities that keep the programs and ministries running. When people expend a lot of energy on irrelevant tasks, burnout can occur. Periodic reviews (I recommend twice yearly) ensure that the church is on track with its overall mission. I review each staff person at my church every six months. The first review is a progress report on how they are achieving annual goals. The second is an annual review of job performance.

Maintaining agreed-upon personal standards encourages integrity. Our pastors and elders proactively established for ourselves five main areas of accountability.[6] You may choose to revise or add to these standards, but they are a good starting point to ensure that all pastors, elders, and ministry leaders avoid situations that might lead to compromise or the appearance of compromise.

1. *Appropriate relationships:* Pastors and elders will exercise prudence when meeting alone with others and avoid any potentially compromising situations.
2. *Accountability partners:* Every pastor and elder will have at least one accountability partner with whom they regularly communicate.
3. *Internet tracking:* Every pastor and elder will have some form of internet tracking installed on their personal computers, phones, and other electronic devices—to which their spouse has full access.
4. *Giving:* Pastors and elders will regularly report their giving. All pastors and elders are expected to maintain a healthy level of giving to the church.
5. *Church involvement:* In addition to consistently attending worship services, pastors and elders are expected to be involved in some form of small group (life group, Bible study, etc.) where community can be built.

Though we should certainly have high standards for every church member, most churches will have higher expectations of their paid staff and different accountability measures for staff members than for volunteers. Though some people would like everyone in the church—paid or otherwise—to have the same standards, such an arrangement is unrealistic.

The goal of these accountability standards is to protect church employees while also promoting healthy spiritual growth. But even though some accountability measures may differ between paid staff and volunteers, everyone operates within the same church system. Making this system as cohesive and consistent as possible is a critical part of creating a safe church environment.

## Consistent Systems for Leaders and Volunteers

"I would like to lead a small group in my home."

"I'm ready to serve in the children's ministry."

"I have a desire to teach high school students."

"I would love to sing in the choir."

"My calling is to communicate the eschatological implications of pre-Tribulation, pre-millennial dispensationalism according to the apocalyptic prophecies of the Bible."

As a lead pastor, I have heard all of these. But what is the proper way to respond? Every ministry of the church needs a consistent system for qualifying, training, and equipping leaders. In short, we must treat every potential leader the same way. Once someone becomes a leader, they must be held accountable by the same system. Judging by personal or family reputation, playing favorites, giving someone a pass, or looking the other way creates an environment in which predators thrive and people who are so inclined can take advantage of the church. For instance, through my work as a consultant, I have encountered several embezzlement cases that arose because the church did not have adequate financial systems in place.

Effective systems must include standards and procedures for identifying, qualifying, and training new leaders, volunteers, and staff members; maintaining clear and consistent communication; and if necessary, removing a leader, volunteer, or staff member from a ministry in a fair, firm, and impartial way.

Recruiting and training leaders for the first impressions ministry may look different from the system you will use for the children's ministry. The key is to maintain uniform standards for all volunteers. Consider the following questions before handing over the keys—literally or figuratively—to a volunteer in any area of ministry:

1. Is the person a member of the church?
2. How long have they been a member?
3. Does the person support the church financially?
4. Does the person prayerfully support the pastors and elders?
5. Does the person agree with essential church doctrine?
6. Has the person demonstrated a pattern of faithful attendance at church?

Once your ministry teams are in place, you should communicate with everyone in a regular and consistent manner. We send weekly emails and text messages to inform leaders of upcoming events and other things they need to know.

Every leader receives these messages at the same time. One thing I learned very quickly as a lead pastor is that I cannot communicate in person faster than people can text their interpretation. Even as I'm speaking, anyone in the room can message someone else before I finish my sentence. A consistent pattern of communication will help to minimize the fallout from the telephone game.

Standards and procedures for removing a leader or a volunteer worker are often missing from a church's ministry leadership system. Sometimes a leader must step down for disciplinary reasons. Or they might have a personal problem and need to *receive* ministry rather than give it. Does a leader need a short break, or is the situation more serious? When there are problems, do not let a leader float from one ministry to another. Such transfers are rife with dangers—for leaders and the people around them. Deal with the problems in an up-front way and clearly communicate the pathway back to a leadership position—if such a return is in everyone's best interest. Depending on the severity and nature of the problem, returning to leadership might not be advised. Indeed, some moral failures warrant permanent disqualification from church leadership.

Without consistent systems, churches inevitably play favorites and overlook problems. A good system will include responses to a range of issues—from unintended human error to impure motives to willful sin. No system is foolproof, but it is the height of foolishness to operate church ministries without a basic system of training, maintaining, and removing leaders and volunteers.

## Work *with* the System, Not around It

The look on the bookkeeper's face was all I needed to see. She was about to give me some bad news.

"What's the damage?" I asked.

"I have no idea."

"That is not what I wanted to hear."

Dawn is an expert bookkeeper, exceptionally knowledgeable about churches and nonprofits. I had asked her to examine the books of an association of churches because of an overdraft at the bank. Every month, the churches contributed financially to the association, which was a separate nonprofit entity. The money was intended to aid local churches in working together on special projects. Though few special projects had yet been undertaken, the expected balance of funds was not in the checking account.

"The front office assistant has force-balanced the books every month for the past several years," Dawn told me. "Frankly, there is no way to know where this money has gone."

"Do you suspect embezzlement?" I asked.

"She says she doesn't like the financial policies but claims she didn't take any money."

I wish stories like this were rare. Unfortunately, similar situations occur often in churches and small nonprofits with limited oversight. In this case, the front office assistant decided to work around the system rather than submit to it. Did she take the money? We will never know. Though a system of checks and balances had been established, the bookkeeper had neglected to follow proper procedure—and there was no accountability.

How can you be part of the solution in your church and not part of the problem? The best thing you can do is submit to the same system as everyone else, even if you would like to change parts of it. Finding work-arounds creates holes in the process and may foster a culture of mistrust. Churches are much safer when all leaders, staff, and volunteers adhere to the same system. Every time someone works around the system, the church becomes less secure.

## The Letter of the Law vs. the Spirit of the Law

When Pastor John walked into the sanctuary for the Sunday evening business meeting, he knew that trouble was brewing. The room was full of people who had not attended church in months. One person in particular caught John's attention. George was an expert in *Robert's Rules of Order*, a parliamentary procedure many churches use to govern business meetings. John noticed a contingent of people seated around George. Many of them had left the church a few months earlier, and John thought they were in the process of joining another church. He was wrong. They had spent the intervening time plotting a takeover, and they appeared to have enough people present to succeed.

George's goal at the meeting was to force a vote on John's removal as pastor. He understood how to leverage the bylaws and parliamentary procedure to twist the meeting in his favor. Thankfully, enough people at the meeting saw through the machinations and voted to retain John.

In this case, George leveraged the letter of the law to violate the spirit of the law. The church at large did not want to remove John as pastor, but the letter of the law allowed it. Following the letter of the law means adhering strictly to what is written. The spirit of the law refers to the perceived purpose of the law and the underlying reasons why the law was written in the first place. Both are important.

The distinction between the letter of the law and the spirit of the law is crucial when we're making ethical decisions. It's necessary to understand the literal interpretation of legal documents such as church bylaws. But it's equally important to understand the purpose, intent, and practical application of those same bylaws. Church bylaws cannot account for every possible scenario—at least not without becoming unwieldy.

When might the spirit of the law trump the letter of the law?

In our church, for example, we have a bathroom reserved for children in the kids' hall. The signage is clear and bold. The letter of the law says that no adults are to use the kids' bathroom. The intent of the sign is to protect the children's safety. We turn adults away on Sundays when they attempt to go in there. Now, let's assume one of our facility volunteers is painting a room at the church one afternoon when no children are present, and the paint fumes make him feel queasy. Without paying much attention, he goes into the kids' restroom to splash water on his face. Should we enact discipline on him? Of course not. In this situation, the spirit of the law would supersede the letter of the law. Common sense would prevail. A safe church discerns when the spirit of the law outweighs the letter of the law.

## When a Black Swan Lands

On April 18, 2008, the community where we lived in southern Indiana was rattled by a magnitude 5.2 earthquake. The area had minimal damage: a collapsed front porch, some crumbled bricks, and fallen masonry.[7] The earthquake could be described as a "Black Swan" event, an unpredictable outlier that has a broad impact on people. Black Swan events are completely unexpected and have an effect on a large group. The name is derived from a long-held belief that all swans were white—a belief that prevailed until somebody saw a black one.[8]

One of the more notable Black Swans in recent history was the pandemic of 2020. The entire world felt the impact, and no one predicted it. While a checklist may help facilitate ordinary operations, by definition, little can be done to prepare for Black Swans. When a Black Swan lands, how do you respond? No checklist will solve the problem. Still, you can include language in your governing documents giving certain people authority to act. Contracts often have *force majeure* language, which refers to a "superior or irresistible force," or "an event or effect that cannot be reasonably anticipated or controlled," for which no party can be held accountable.[9] After the pandemic, our church adopted the following language in our bylaws: "In the case of a *force majeure* event, the lead pastor will work with the church council to make decisions on behalf of the church."

Most likely, you will encounter only a few Black Swan events in a lifetime of ministry, but almost every issue of church safety is *predictable*. Sexual, physical, and emotional abuse issues are *not* Black Swans. Unfortunately, they happen. But you can be prepared. Indeed, I believe churches are a huge part of the solution to this massive cultural problem.

# THE SYSTEMIC PROBLEM
# OF ABUSE

A spiritual war raged in the heavens when Christ Jesus was born. That same war continues on earth today, and we and our children are potential casualties. Revelation 12 describes how Satan, depicted as a large red dragon, wanted to devour the baby Jesus—a far cry from the familiar, serene nativity story in Luke 2, where Mary snugly wraps the newborn babe in cloths as lowly shepherds worship and an angel announces good news of great joy for all people. If Luke 2 is the hand-bell version of Christ's birth, then Revelation 12 is the heavy metal version. Luke's account describes what happened in the seen world, while John's account in Revelation reveals the spiritual war behind the scenes.

The dragon in Revelation 12 is the ancient serpent of Genesis. At the beginning of human history, Satan lied to Eve, telling her she would not die if she followed his instructions. Both Adam and Eve fell into Satan's trap, but God already had a plan in place to redeem them, and their descendants, from their sin. In Genesis 3:15, we learn that an offspring of Eve—later revealed as the Christ child—would crush the serpent's head, defeat evil, and redeem humanity. Throughout the Old Testament, Satan was on the prowl, waiting for the advent of this promised child. Not knowing God's timing, the devil took the lives of as many children as possible, hoping he might kill the Messiah before the plan of redemption could be completed.

Who is the woman giving birth in pain and agony in Revelation 12? Perhaps she is Mary, the mother of Jesus, who gave physical birth to Christ on earth. More likely, the woman represents the nation of Israel, characterized at times in the Old Testament as a mother giving birth, agonizing and suffering for centuries, waiting for the Messiah to be born. In this story, we see how God promised redemption when he promised a baby. The incarnation of Jesus was a culmination in the war against Satan, as God's promise to ransom captive Israel and save the world through Immanuel began coming to fruition on earth.

We learn in Revelation that Satan tried to stop the birth of Christ. He even took a third of heaven's angels with him in the process. These fallen angels now wage war alongside Satan, but they are no match for Jesus. Still, since the beginning of time, Satan has tried to harm children. In Exodus, he wanted Pharaoh to murder baby Hebrew boys. In Esther, he wanted Haman to commit genocide against the Jews—including children. And in Matthew's Gospel, he wanted Herod to kill baby Jesus. Why? The dragon wanted to murder the Messiah before he could come of age. Failing that, he retaliated against all boys under the age of two in the vicinity of Bethlehem.[1] He attacks people of all ages, of course, but Satan is particularly vicious against children, the most vulnerable among us. He wants to kill them in the womb, confuse their identities, and steal their innocence. Even more alarming, Satan sends predators to attack our young ones at every opportunity. The threats are real, ongoing, and large-scale. The infection of evil is systemic, not localized, on earth.

## Why Systemic Abuse Exists

Sexual, physical, and emotional abuse are widespread problems not limited to churches.[2] Unfortunately, many organizations have systems and cultures where predators are not held accountable, or may even go unnoticed. When Rachael Denhollander spoke out about her abuser, Larry Nassar, a once-respected doctor for the USA women's gymnastics team, she wondered whether anyone would listen. Thankfully, they did, and her courageous story helped countless victims.[3] Another victim of abuse, Christa Brown, described how her story was largely ignored for years by the Southern Baptist Convention. She wrote about how "dreadful safety gaps" led to "an institutionalized inertia that cloaks evil behind a veil of denial and leaves countless kids at risk."[4] Unfortunately, these stories are not rare exceptions.

The roots of abuse are found in the soil of a sinful desire for power and influence. Abuse happens because power prevails. Power gives abusers the freedom to act, and as power grows, so does the frequency and intensity of abuse.[5] Power may be real or only perceived, but abusers often have legitimate authority over their victims. Victimizers use various forms of control to silence their victims' voices.[6] Emotional power can be used to intimidate and silence. Physical power can be used to subdue. Economic power can be used to manipulate and control. Verbal power uses words to establish influence over someone. Why does abuse exist in churches? Because churches are notorious for having power structures without accountability. Spiritual abusers appear to build God's Kingdom but are motivated by their own quest for power and authority.[7]

The word *systemic* refers to problems that pervade an overall system or culture. These problems are not isolated or infrequent but are relatively widespread. They persist because of inherent flaws that go unaddressed. For example, one in seven children in the United States has experienced some form of abuse or neglect in the past year.[8] Additionally, 41 percent of women and 26 percent of men have experienced sexual violence, physical violence, and/or stalking by an intimate partner.[9] The problem of abuse is everywhere, and our churches are not only not immune, but they may be particularly vulnerable because of the level of trust people have in the institution.

Though it's hard to obtain precise statistics substantiating the number of cases of sexual abuse in the church, we know that insurance companies handle hundreds of claims a year in which a pastor, staff person, or volunteer is accused of such abuse.[10] The problem is every bit as real in the church as it is in the larger culture. We live in a hypersexual culture in which children are exposed to a repeated and perverse narrative. Pastors and church leaders who ignore these issues are guilty of disregarding one of the most dangerous problems affecting children. Churches must be vigilant because spiritual darkness is everywhere.

## Why Churches Are Targets

The biggest mistake we can make is to assume that abuse won't happen in our churches. "It can't happen here" is a dangerously naive statement. Any organization with children and other vulnerable people is a target for predators. Satan especially wants to attack churches, and he loves to destroy children. In practice, predators seek out places with low security, high levels of grace and trust, and a significant presence of children. Most churches seek to treat people with hospitality rather than suspicion. Unlike most public schools or other youth-oriented organizations, a stranger can walk into a church and receive a big welcome. John 10:10 warns that spiritual thieves steal, kill, and destroy. Predators steal the innocence of children and other vulnerable people. Predators subvert the mission of the church and destroy the lives of families.

What if something happens at your church? Because most churches will experience some form of attack, you must be prepared with specific policies and procedures to create a safe environment and reduce the opportunity for abuse. Every staff member and volunteer must understand the process for identifying and reporting abuse. Report every reasonable suspicion of abuse or neglect to the proper authorities. Avoid a scandal by handling situations of abuse quickly, honestly, and straightforwardly. A cover-up will cause just as much harm as the offense.

We will examine these issues more comprehensively in chapters 5 and 6. For now, I want to establish that proper policies and procedures are necessary to protect the vulnerable in your church. You must also allocate enough *resources* to implement these policies and procedures. I understand that budgetary constraints are a considerable factor in churches, but safety must be given priority. If your church must choose between purchasing adult curriculum and paying for background checks, the safety of the children must come first. If your church must decide between a new choir room and creating safer areas for Sunday school and day care, the safety of the children must come first. Child protection is far too important to become an afterthought in the church budget. It should be among the top ministry priorities for your church.

Where might systemic flaws in your church's culture create gaps where predators can gain access? Consider home groups. Most churches have specific processes for ensuring on-campus child safety during regular church hours. A greater danger may involve church-sanctioned events and programs that are held off-site. In-home Bible studies and small groups are particularly susceptible to lax controls. Many of the worst cases of child abuse have occurred in home groups. Too often I hear of home groups in which children are placed in a room with limited or no supervision. If that were to happen at church on Sunday morning, most parents would be shocked. Off-campus and in-home groups, by virtue of their private setting, should have even tighter controls than on-campus public gatherings. Predators often gravitate to the most trusting environments with the most lenient supervision. Unfortunately, many home groups typify this environment.

What should we do about suspected abusers? One of the most difficult aspects of church safety involves people we suspect have the potential to harm someone but who have not acted out yet. Obviously, we shouldn't be overly suspicious or wrongly accuse someone. Spreading mistrust without supporting facts is not helpful and can cause much damage. However, neglecting certain signs that raise suspicions is equally dangerous. More than 90 percent of victims under the age of eighteen know their abuser.[11] Is it possible that a disheveled stranger will dash into your church and snatch a child? It's possible, but not likely. Almost every case of abuse in churches occurs after bonds of trust have been formed over time. Predators use trust as a tactic as much as brute force. As with any sin issue, pastors and church leaders should talk to an individual if suspicions arise. It is better to have an awkward conversation and maintain a safe environment than dismiss suspicions and experience a tragedy.

## Recognizing Where Abuse Begins

Abuse originates in the way victimizers view others. At some level they believe other people exist to fulfill their desires. People who take advantage of others place themselves at the center and try to control the orbits of vulnerable people around them. Victimizers are not necessarily brash or over-powering. They may be sensitive, subdued, and even charming. Many abusers have likable personalities. So what are some warning signs to watch for?

*Entitlement:* "I deserve your attention." When abusers fail to get someone's attention, they will penalize the other person through aggressive tactics such as yelling, name-calling, throwing objects, or worse.[12] They believe their time is more valuable than someone else's. This mindset creates agitation when they don't receive the time and attention they desire or think they deserve.

*Superiority:* "I am always right." Abusers believe their feelings and opinions are more important than someone else's, and they may manipulate, coerce, or demand others to see things the same way. You rarely hear abusers admit to being wrong, and they offer insincere apologies, if any at all. It's always "I'm sorry, *but* . . . I'm sorry *if* . . . I'm sorry, *however* . . ." Such statements aren't apologies; they are posturing to assert superiority over someone else.

*Duplicity:* "I do not need to follow the rules." When abusers have formal authority, they create rules for their subordinates but not themselves. They enforce standards on everyone else to make themselves feel superior. For example, a senior pastor might require a camera in everyone's office but his own. Or he might mandate computer tracking software for other staff members but not himself.

*Justification:* "My anger is warranted." There are times when it's appropriate to be angry, such as when facing injustice, unfairness, or duplicity. But abusers don't get angry when someone else experiences injustice. Instead, their rage comes to a boil when their own desires, demands, or expectations are unmet. It's a selfish form of anger. Often, abusers have "lonely anger," meaning no one else shares their feelings. As such, victimizers feel the need to justify their anger. They force people to agree with them to validate their own feelings.

*Manipulation:* "That didn't happen." "You're overreacting." "Your questions are attacking me." Invalidation is a classic method of manipulation that attempts to make other people doubt their own perceptions or experiences in favor of the abuser's perspective. The goal of invalidation is to gain power and control over someone else. When questioned, victimizers often use invalidating to get others to doubt themselves.

Most people, myself included, have used one or more of these tactics at one time or another. We're sinners, after all.

So don't play gotcha games with people. We all have bad moments, days, or weeks, and at times we may resort to some of these negative behaviors. But a *regular pattern* of behavior in someone that includes several of these warning signs should raise concerns. Does a discernable pattern mean someone is an abuser? No, but we should be cautious, especially if the person is around vulnerable people in the church.

## Internal Threats: Wolves and Predators

In 2019, the *Houston Chronicle* published a six-part investigation into the Southern Baptist Convention, concerning hundreds of abusers who were leaders of churches—with more than seven hundred victims over two decades across thirty states.[13] I remember reading the stories with disgust. Many of these predators were allowed to move from church to church and abuse even more people. The horrors originated within churches. The threat was internal, not external.

There is a difference between a predator and a wolf. A predator may come from anywhere. But the Bible gives a special warning about wolves—namely, church leaders who look the part but are dangerous. Matthew records this warning from Jesus: "Beware of false prophets who come disguised as harmless sheep but are really vicious wolves. You can identify them by their fruit, that is, by the way they act."[14]

Wolves are inclined to do as much damage to the church as possible. The carnage may come in the form of false teaching or bad doctrine. But it can also take the form of abuse.

Wolves are "disguised as harmless" and often go undetected. How can you recognize them? Look for the fruit—watch the way they act. Do they exhibit entitlement, superiority, duplicity, justification, and manipulation? I believe churches are more prepared to handle external threats from predators than they are to confront internal threats from wolves.

Anyone can be the target of abuse. But you must also consider how people become victimizers. I believe anyone is capable of any sin at any time. That may sound extreme, but the moment we start thinking we're immune to certain sins, we become vulnerable and can find ourselves in a lot of trouble. Consider the life of Judas Iscariot, the disciple who betrayed Jesus.

Jesus chose Judas as a disciple, but Judas chose betrayal over salvation. There is nothing extraordinary about Judas's darkness. He likely became a follower of Jesus because he recognized the Lord's power, especially his ability to perform miracles. But Judas had his own agenda. He did not submit to Christ spiritually. He cared more for his own political ambition than for Kingdom salvation. What was at the core of Judas's betrayal? He saw Jesus as a means to an end. We're all susceptible to this kind of darkness.

In the garden of Gethsemane, Judas approached Jesus with a mob and betrayed him with a kiss.[15] It was a standard greeting in that culture, but this kiss was filled with false intimacy. A sign of affection became a means of betrayal.

Judas was the opposite of Jesus in the garden. In effect, he was saying, "Not your will, God, but mine." Judas shows that proximity to Jesus does not save us. You can be *in* church and entirely *out* of God's Kingdom. We don't know exactly why Judas did what he did. The Bible doesn't tell us. But reading his story should cause us to examine our own hearts for the seeds of betrayal. Are we guilty of false intimacy? Are we in close proximity to Jesus in the church but far away from him spiritually? Are we pursuing our own agenda and willing to do what it takes—including betrayal—to get what we think we want?

Safe churches are keenly aware of the external threat from predators. But even more, safe churches are willing to root out and eliminate the internal threat from wolves.

4

# SECURING YOUR PHYSICAL CAMPUS

Jenny, our family minister, pulled me aside between worship services.

"We found a lost child," she said. There was a mix of panic and relief in her voice, and I was confused.

"Is everything okay?"

"There was a preschooler in our parking lot, and we have no idea where his parents are."

I had to lead the second service, so I left the follow-up in Jenny's capable hands. But after the service, I darted over to the children's hall and found her.

"We located the parents," she said.

"What happened?"

Jenny explained that our parking team had found a young child walking alone. They took him to our children's ministry area, thinking he must have somehow managed to walk out an open door. None of the volunteers recognized the child and noticed he did not have a check-in tag on his back. They quickly figured out he was from the neighborhood.

"The boy is safe," Jenny explained, "but I sent out dozens of people to walk the neighborhood to find his parents."

I was there for the reunification with the mother. As you can expect, she was filled with joy. In a fluke accident, the young preschooler had found a way out of his fenced backyard and started walking. He covered about a half mile before wandering into our parking lot. Because our internal systems secure all children on our campus, our parking volunteers were able to quickly recognize a child in danger.

Campus security means more than preparing for potential violence. Indeed, you are more likely to encounter a lost child on your campus than an armed threat. Without a good system in place, a child wandering in the parking lot might create a lot of confusion. Because we have a mandatory check-in system and a watchful security team, we were able to recognize what was happening relatively quickly. When you properly secure the church campus, you equip your volunteers to respond to a variety of incidents that may occur at any given time.

How can you prepare your church for the unpredictable? No plan is foolproof, but you can reduce risk dramatically with the right approach. The following nine commitments will go a long way toward establishing greater security on your church campus.

## Commitment 1: We Are Consistent

Different churches will have different policies and procedures to ensure safety. A *policy* is a formal rule that undergirds comprehensive standards. *Procedures* are operational instructions used to implement policies. For example, your church will likely have a policy of performing background checks on any volunteer working with minors. The procedure is the process by which this background check occurs. Policies are the *what*, and procedures are the *how*. The key to safety is *consistency*. Policies and procedures are worthless unless they apply to everyone.

Pam is a preschool director in the Florida Panhandle. I recently took a tour of the church campus where the preschool meets. As a guest, I had to wear a specific name tag and be escorted by an approved staff person through every area where there were children. This policy applies to everyone. As we walked through one area, my guide unlocked and immediately relocked each door. They had a clear policy that all guests must be accompanied. The procedures included keeping all doors locked and not leaving visitors unattended.

Consistency means no exceptions, even for top leaders such as the lead pastor. My children's minister came to me recently and said it was time to renew my background check.

Did I push back and pull rank because I'm the lead pastor? No. I gladly submitted to the same guidelines as everyone else. Every exception is one step closer to danger.

## Commitment 2: We Are Equipped

I watched the elderly gentleman sway as I preached. He was one of our older members and also one of our best dressed. Every week, he looked incredibly dapper, sometimes sporting a hat that looked like it was from the 1940s—which was entirely possible since the man was in his nineties. Suddenly, he fell from his seat and collapsed onto the floor.

A nearby church member, a nurse, immediately sprang into action. As she reached his side, the man lifted his arm straight into the air as he continued lying on the floor.

"I'm all right, everyone!" he said loudly. "I just fell asleep."

My team still laughs when someone recounts that story. Thankfully, what happened that day wasn't serious. But in my twenty years of preaching, I have witnessed three medical emergencies during Sunday services. In each case, the congregation was prepared to respond. We've had someone with heart issues and someone with seizures. Then there was the time a boy accidentally lit his younger sister's hair on fire during the Christmas Eve candlelight service.

A secure church campus involves both safety and medical preparedness. You are far more likely to have a medical emergency than an active shooter. Your church should have and maintain basic first aid kits and AEDs throughout your facility (including having pediatric pads for the AED nearest the children's area). As well, key volunteers should be trained and equipped to provide CPR. A process should be in place for parents to alert volunteers about a child's allergies. A safe church is always equipped with the right resources to respond to potential emergencies. Remember, "training is a perishable skill," meaning it loses effectiveness when not utilized.[1] You must continue to train your volunteers even if your policies and procedures do not change.

### Commitment 3: We Are Aware

"Where did the MacBook go?" a worship volunteer asked.

"Not again," I mumbled.

For several weeks in a row, we had experienced a string of thefts at the church. Someone even had the gall to roll a large flat-screen television and cart right out the front door of our foyer. A group of thieves had targeted us because of our lack of surveillance cameras and because we had doors that could easily be opened even when locked. To be clear, this happened at a previous church of mine and both problems have long since been solved.

Churches are often targets because of the nature of accessibility in our facilities. People dump stolen vehicles in church parking lots, knowing they will often go unnoticed for days. The trusting environment in a church causes people to let down their guard. A crime of opportunity occurs when a perpetrator takes advantage of a situation, often without planning or forethought. Someone sees an unattended laptop or tablet and snags it.

Safe churches have a heightened sense of awareness. You've likely read or heard the phrase, "If you *see* something, *say* something." The New York Metropolitan Transportation Authority implemented the slogan after the terrorist attacks on September 11, 2001, and it has since been adopted in a variety of places. The purpose of the campaign is to help people *recognize* suspicious behavior and know how to *report* it to proper authorities.[2] Odd behavior should draw the attention of volunteers, and churches should create a culture where reporting this behavior to the right leaders is not only appropriate but expected.[3] Will you have false alarms? Yes. Most reports will probably amount to nothing. But creating a culture of awareness is worth the effort of dealing with false alarms.

## Commitment 4: We Are Prepared

Hurricanes are a way of life in Florida. My church is close to the coast, and a large storm will threaten our area every few years. We have procedures in place for responding to tropical storms, including when to cancel activities. Only twice have we had to cancel Sunday morning services. You may not have hurricanes in your area, but almost every part of North America has the potential to be affected by a natural disaster.

When I pastored in Indiana, we had a contract for snow removal and plans to deal with large ice storms. At my church in Kentucky, we had a designated place for people to go during tornado warnings. I remember everyone in the church huddling in a hallway one Wednesday night while a storm passed. We were prepared, and thankfully no damage occurred. When danger makes a surprise appearance, our brains revert to *normalcy bias*—the innate belief that everything will continue as normal, which can cause us to dismiss a threat and minimize a crisis rather than accept reality and respond with urgency.[4] This psychological mechanism may explain why some people who hear gunshots may think they are hearing fireworks, or why some people interpret screams as playful laughter.

Safe churches have basic plans in place for natural disasters and other events in which communication is critical. My church utilizes a text system and can message our entire congregation if needed. Though we rarely need to take such a step, we have, on occasion, sent a text to everyone informing them of an important change of plans. I'm grateful that our "message read" rates are close to 100 percent. We are prepared if necessary.

## Commitment 5: We Are Cautious

There was a time when we had to file an insurance claim to cover medical expenses after someone tripped over an extension cord. To this day, I have no idea how the incident happened. The cord ran behind a table and was not in an area where people typically walked. The person's explanation made no sense to me, but it didn't matter. From that point on, we became more cautious about basic safety issues.

Safe churches have a heightened sense of caution and take proactive measures to prevent accidents from occurring. Are the hallways clear? Is the children's area clean? Are stairwells properly lit? Caution involves common sense. If a light in the parking lot goes out, replace it promptly. If a faucet leaks, fix it. Carelessness or neglect almost always costs more in the long run.

## Commitment 6: We Are Watchful

I once posted a video on social media of a car doing dough-nuts in our church parking lot. My motivation was two-fold. First, I wanted to identify the culprit, but I was also impressed with the driver's ability to leave massive tire marks on the asphalt. It didn't take long for our neighbors to recognize the muscle car and point us to the most likely suspect. We visited the young man's house and told him he was always welcome at our church, so long as he didn't perform burn-outs on his way out.

The cost of security cameras has dropped dramatically in recent years, and every church should have them in critical areas. A safe church is a watchful church. Safety and security are an ongoing concern, and cameras can help you monitor what happens on your campus.[5] If an incident occurs, having cameras in your church is an excellent way to determine the truth about what happened and who was involved.

## Commitment 7: We Are Current

A few years ago, we started tackling facility projects. Our church had done very few updates in the last forty years, and now we had to complete several fixes all at once. Thankfully, the congregation rallied, and we raised the needed funds to address the most immediate problems. But we're still playing catch-up today because, for too long, deferred maintenance was not a budget priority.

Deferred maintenance refers to putting off needed infrastructure improvements because of budget and cash limitations. Churches are notorious for postponing capital projects. We recently heard of a church that had worn their carpet through to the plywood floor. But rather than replace the carpet, they painted the wood floor the same color as the surrounding carpet. When you make these shortsighted fixes, the cost of collective repairs skyrockets.

Neglected facilities become an albatross around the neck of many churches. Deferred maintenance has thwarted many pastors' best intentions. Even the most up-to-date church facilities often have closets full of junk—old trophies, dusty puppets, and binders of music from the 1970s. In severe cases, the entire campus has not been touched in decades. Failing air conditioners, leaky roofs, unsealed brick exteriors, old windows, and worn carpets can potentially sink a congregation. Redoing the central air conditioning of a 50,000-square-foot facility can easily cost more than one million dollars. Sealing brick exteriors can cost tens of thousands of dollars. The cost of repairing a leaky roof can climb into six figures if a lot of work is needed.

Church facilities are one of the most expensive—yet vital—tools that church leaders use to shepherd God's people. In a North American context, buildings are essential to God's mission of expanding his Kingdom. A safe church makes the needed sacrifices to keep its facilities current.

## Commitment 8: We Are Calm

"He just started walking toward me while I preached."

A pastor was describing to me what happened during a recent Sunday service.

"No one quite knew what to do, so I stopped preaching and conversed with him."

Apparently, the man had mental health issues and was unaware of social norms. He was not a threat, but he was disruptive. Nonviolent disruptions are relatively common and will happen occasionally in churches. The goal is to remain calm and remove the person from the meeting as quickly and quietly as possible. Once that has happened, you can further assess the situation and offer assistance or take appropriate steps to remove the person from the church campus. But churches are not obligated to tolerate someone who is disrupting on-campus activities.

We once had a person try to put political flyers on the windshields of vehicles in our parking lot. In this case, our first impressions team removed the flyers before the end of the service and told the man that what he was doing wasn't allowed. In rare cases, a disruptive person may attempt to return to the church. If this happens, call the police and let them handle the situation. A church can also request a court order barring someone from the church campus. Violators can be found in contempt of court. A safe church remains calm and doesn't escalate a disruptive situation.

## Commitment 9: We Are Quick

You should certainly be quick to report any suspicions of child endangerment to the proper authorities. But being quick also means being ready to respond to sudden threats that arise.

Churches are considered "soft" target because their campuses are often easily accessible and are generally unprotected. Additionally, churches are vulnerable because they are open to the public, and guests are not typically challenged or questioned.[6] The likelihood is low that you will experience something like an active shooter, but you still must be prepared.[7] Active shooter situations are often over within ten to fifteen minutes and before law enforcement can arrive.[8] Other cases of violence on church campuses also occur rapidly and require a quick response.

Though no single plan of action is possible when preparing for an active shooter or other violence on your campus, what is most important is *decisiveness*.[9] You have three immediate options when confronted with a perpetrator of violence: *run*, *hide*, or *fight*.

In the first option, escape is the priority. You should leave behind all personal items, take as many other people as possible with you, and run out of the building. Once you are in a safe place, call 911.

If you cannot escape the situation, the second option is to hide—if possible, in a room with thick walls and few windows. Lock and barricade the doors, turn off the lights, and remain silent.

The third option is to fight the perpetrator. Use anything nearby, such as a fire extinguisher or a chair, to distract or incapacitate the attacker. Fighting back may seem daunting or impossible, but in some cases it is the best option for surviving an attack. In one study of forty-one active shooter events, potential victims stopped the attacker in sixteen instances before law enforcement arrived.[10]

Whichever response you choose, quick and decisive action can save lives.

Everyone serving in your church should make these nine commitments. Church leaders should invest in ways to enhance the acceptance of these nine commitments by your members. No church is completely free from danger, and no campus can be made perfectly safe. However, a firm commitment to securing the physical campus will considerably reduce potential harm.

5

# PROTECTING AND
# EQUIPPING CHILDREN

Joan, a leader in her church's children's ministry, knew that some kids were hurting because of turmoil in their family. The three siblings regularly mentioned heated arguments between their parents. Though the details were fuzzy, the pain was evident.

Despite the deteriorating situation at home, the family was active weekly in the church. The children's ministry was a lifeline for the parents and a respite for the kids. Church seemed to be the only place where peace prevailed.

So when the family missed three Sundays in a row, Joan called the mother.

"How are you?" she asked. "I haven't seen you and your family in a few weeks, and I wanted to check in with you."

"Things are rough, but I believe they will be okay soon," the mother replied.

"What can I do?" Joan asked. She could tell by the woman's voice that tensions were escalating in the home.

"Nothing right now, but I will let you know."

After the phone call, Joan felt especially burdened to pray for the family. They had never shared specific information, and her concerns led her to seek God for wisdom.

A few weeks later, the mother started bringing her kids to church again, but she only dropped them off and no longer stayed for the worship service. She said nothing about why she and her husband were not attending.

Joan decided to pursue the issue at the next pickup time.

"Please share what you can. How is your family? I hate to push, but I'm concerned."

"Thank you," the woman responded. "Perhaps I can share something soon, but we're still working things out."

The following Sunday, the mother dropped off her kids, and the dad picked them up a little bit early. They ran to him and jumped into his arms. As Joan watched, she thought, *Maybe they are beginning to heal.*

A few minutes later, the mother arrived. She seemed startled when she didn't see the children.

"Your husband picked them up already," Joan said.

The mom's horrified scream stopped her cold.

"His parental rights were just terminated!" she said. "They've been kidnapped."

We often associate child abduction with shadowy strangers

and nefarious villains. And of course the church should be concerned about potential predators. But the greater danger often exists in the familiar. The circumstances in Joan's case were difficult to discern, but the threat was very real. And it's one that churches face whenever children are on campus.

## Ten Nonnegotiable Rules for Child Safety

Child security is one of the most important discipleship issues in the church. We must create robust security measures in our churches, making our campuses internally safe for children so they can grow to spiritual maturity and become equipped to confront the dangers of evil in the world.

What happened with Joan was a system failure, not a personal failure. She did everything correctly—she was involved, she cared, she called, she prayed—but there was a flaw in the checkout process—namely, that family members were allowed to pick up children even if they hadn't dropped them off.

Millions of people volunteer in church children's ministries every week. Most care deeply about the children and wouldn't hesitate to make great personal sacrifices to protect them. When your church has a proper system of protection, you mitigate the risks and help your leaders discern when personal failures occur that must be addressed.

In September 2023, I had conversations with Jenny Smith, a curriculum and content developer for Awana with decades of ministry experience serving in children's ministry, and Dr. Pam Whitaker, senior vice president of program development at One More Child, where she develops new, innovative programming to serve vulnerable children and struggling families. I am grateful for the insight of these two ministry professionals, who helped me identify the following best practices for building better child-safety systems in our churches.[1]

### 1. Never be alone with a child who is not your own

You might never do anything to harm a child, but a lot of things can go wrong when you are alone with a child who is not your own. Always seek help when anything questionable arises. "I don't want to bother anyone with this issue" is not an excuse. Yes, *most of the time* you can handle a problem with a child without involving others. But churches and volunteers must always be prepared for those instances that happen *some of the time*. It is better to have a fast and firm policy that ministry leaders, staff members, and volunteers are never to be alone with a child than to have a system in which people are making situational decisions about whether or when it's okay. The best policy is to require that at least two people always be present with a child.

### 2. Background checks for everyone, every year

Though background screening will only catch those who have been caught before, it is still a critical part of any good safety plan. If you loosen this standard, you create an environment that may attract people who desire to harm a child. Your church becomes an easier target. Background checks are less about *catching* someone and more about *deterring* the wrong people from your ministry. The best practice is to renew the screening annually for anyone who serves in any capacity around children, even if only for a short time (such as a weeklong Vacation Bible School). All background checks should also be cross-referenced with the national sex offender database.

### 3. Establish a six-month rule for all volunteers

Potential volunteers should demonstrate a faithful pattern of commitment to the church for at least six months before serving in the children's ministry. And not just six months of church attendance, but six months or more of becoming known by others in the congregation. No matter how much your children's ministry might need volunteers, do not give a new church member immediate access to minors. The purpose of this rule is to prevent potential predators—who typically prefer quick access to their victims—from targeting your church. Many predators will not wait for extended periods and will move on to other places where access is easier and more immediate.[2]

### 4. One-on-one conversations with every potential volunteer

Before serving with children, each volunteer should have an informal interview with a trusted leader or staff member. The purpose of these conversations is to look for any red flags or potential concerns. People who are dedicated to child safety will not push back on this step. Good volunteers will be glad the church has a vigorous system of safety and will gladly adhere to this guideline.

### 5. Simple and nonnegotiable check-in and checkout procedures

A common but effective process involves printing two matching tags at check-in. One tag sticks on a child's back between the shoulders (so they can't tear it off). The other tag goes with the parent who checks the child in. No one can pick up the child without the matching tag. This system protects children not only from random strangers but also from the more common problem of being taken by an unauthorized person whom the child knows.

### 6. One-foot-in, one-foot-out bathroom supervision

Every child will likely need a bathroom break at some point on Sunday. Your system should account for children moving through the halls and into the bathroom. No adult should ever be alone with a child in a bathroom. If possible, dedicate specific bathrooms on your campus for children only. Keep these bathroom doors open at all times. Require adults who accompany children to the bathroom to stand at the threshold of the door with one foot inside the bathroom and the other foot outside the bathroom. This way, volunteers can easily speak to the child in the bathroom while maintaining visibility to others.

### 7. Use floaters and management-by-walking-around

The more levels of accountability you have, the better. One way to add a layer of security is to assign floaters to walk between classrooms and down the halls. The presence of floaters provides accountability, and their responsibilities include observing activities, checking on teachers, listening to problems, reporting issues, and providing appropriate solutions to volunteer questions.

### 8. Install safety mechanisms such as cameras and signs

What are the observable environmental safety issues on your church campus? Is a certain room or stairwell too dark? Do you need alarms or buzzers on doors to alert teachers when they are opened? Do you have clear signage for those who need to exit the building? With the availability of inexpensive cameras, almost every church can afford to install a monitoring system in key areas. People will feel safer when they see these visible safety improvements, and you will also deter potential harm.

### 9. Practice ongoing training

Every children's ministry volunteer should receive additional training throughout the year. Information you might cover in these training sessions includes playground safety, first aid tips, trauma-informed care, fire and emergency evacuation routes, allergic reaction prevention measures, classroom management, bullying prevention, and hygiene helps. Church leaders should conduct an annual audit of the church's safety systems. Invite someone outside your ministry to poke holes in your processes, and use the feedback to shore up any weak areas. Regular evaluation ensures a safer church environment.

### 10. Put all important policies in writing

Many churches fail in their safety efforts not because of a lack of concern but because of a lack of *consistency*. Formalize and publish your policies, distribute them to volunteers, and review them regularly. Top church leaders should guide this process. A culture of safety will never develop if loose standards exist and expectations are not made explicit. When an incident occurs, your church should have a template for documenting what happened. Consider distributing a one-page checklist that contains instructions for "Who should I contact if . . . ?" Keep the checklist updated and let your volunteers know you expect them to use it when needed.

Remember, the primary objective of children's ministry is to equip children to be ready for a challenging world in which spiritual warfare is quite real. Should church be fun for kids? Yes, absolutely! But safety and discipleship are the greater goals. As a church leader, you are responsible for keeping children physically, emotionally, and spiritually safe in the church. A safe environment is one in which children can be prepared to face inevitable battles in an unsafe world.

## The Safety Checklist Manifesto

A manifesto is a written declaration of intentions, and a checklist creates a system of accountability. Combine the two and you have an excellent method of maintaining church safety.[3] Airplane pilots run through a checklist before every flight. Do they know how to fly a plane without it? Yes, but the checklist ensures that nothing critical is missed. In ministry, we can easily get distracted by the tyranny of the urgent. But using a checklist, just as an experienced pilot would, ensures that we don't miss something in the moment. A checklist is not a crutch for poor leaders. It is a prudent safety net for regular operations in the church.

How might a checklist work in a children's ministry? Have printed copies available and ask your teachers to arrive five or ten minutes early every Sunday to be prepared. Only the basic operations need to be on the checklist:

- ☐ Are my supplies in place for the lesson?
- ☐ Does every child have a check-in tag?
- ☐ Are there at least two teachers in the room?
- ☐ Did I document attendance?
- ☐ Was every child accompanied to the bathroom?
- ☐ During bathroom breaks, did an adult practice one-foot-in, one-foot-out supervision?
- ☐ During pickup, was every child's check-in tag matched with the corresponding parent tag?

You may want to rework these seven items to apply more specifically to your church. Remember, the checklist is intended to be a quick safety guide, not a comprehensive policy. I would not recommend making the list longer than eight or ten items.

My children are often the last ones to be picked up from our children's ministry after church, because my wife and I end up talking to people after the worship service. I can't tell you how many times I've walked down to the checkout station to pick up my kids only to have to go back to get my wife because she has the check-in tag. Everyone in the church knows who I am and who my four kids are. But there are no exceptions, even for pastors and staff members. The safety checklist manifesto ensures the care of all children and provides a guide for volunteers who desire to uphold high standards.

## Responding When an Incident Occurs

The reality is that no system can mitigate every risk. Something will eventually happen, no matter how careful you are. A child will fall and break an arm on the playground. A teacher might get frustrated and lose composure in a difficult classroom. A child could say something that warrants a call to protective services. Take a moment and consider the huge liability of children's ministry. A child can get lost. A child can get hurt. A child can experience abuse. Sometimes harm occurs unintentionally. For example, a teacher may not be aware of specific food allergies. Unfortunately, some children experience intentional harm. More commonly, injuries occur when one child is too physical with another.

Let me say it one more time: You must be prepared for an incident to occur in your church. It *will* happen eventually. In many situations, it is the lack of an appropriate response, rather than the incident itself, that gets a church in trouble. Three steps are necessary for an appropriate response: *report, record,* and *refer.*[4]

### 1. Report the incident to the proper authorities

I received a call from an out-of-state pastor. He was struggling with the decision to report an incident to child protective services. As we talked, I could tell his church would be significantly affected.

"The person I would report is the husband of our children's minister," he said. His voice cracked as he took deep breaths.

"But you must make the call," I responded.

"Yes, I know," he said. "A child's safety is more important than the church's reputation."

Who is considered a mandatory reporter varies from state to state, as do the circumstances under which a mandatory reporter must make a report. What determines "privileged communication" between clergy and laity also differs by state.[5] Though you should certainly be familiar with the reporting requirements in your area, you should report every reasonable suspicion of abuse and neglect regardless of the guidelines. Do not use the technicalities of the law to shirk your responsibility for protecting children or other vulnerable people. Treat any suspected abuse seriously, report it to the proper authorities, and let them handle it. Church leaders should not act as investigators.[6] Always report an incident immediately and make it your first step.

## 2. Record the details of the incident

Though the investigating authorities will make their own reports, the church should also have a formal way to document incidents. This process should also apply to occurrences that do not rise to the level of notifying outside agencies. For example, we once had a special-needs adult lock himself in a room with a couple of children. Nothing happened, and people were around to deal with the problem quickly. However, we still completed an incident report and carefully documented what had occurred.

## 3. Refer counseling and help to those affected by the incident

When people are hurting, the church should come to their aid, especially if the harm occurred in the church's facilities or during a church event. Offer to pay for professional counseling and other services that can help victims through the healing process. Most churches have a benevolence fund to cover these kinds of costs. If not, you should set one up to be used to help people with a variety of problems, even if the church is not at fault.

God has a plan to change the world with the children of

the church. Let it not be said that we delayed or derailed his plan because of negligence.

You might be wondering what happened in the story at the beginning of the chapter about Joan and the family in turmoil. What did Joan do when she discovered that the children's father had taken them without authorization, and what was the outcome?

Joan reassured the mom and then immediately called the police and explained the situation. She also notified the church's security chief, who quickly dispatched team members to search the campus in case the father and his kids were still there. As two security team members walked the parking lot, they saw the father opening the hood of his car. Perhaps providentially, he was having trouble getting the car started. One of the team members mentioned the summer heat and said he would take the kids inside. The other offered to get jumper cables to start the car. Within minutes, the police arrived, and the kids went home safely with their mother.

After the police took their report, Joan skipped lunch and recorded the details of the event on the church's incident report form. The next day, she called the mother and told her the church would pay for counseling if she and the kids wanted to process what had happened with a professional counselor. The mother should have mentioned the termination of the father's parental rights, but not everyone experiencing a family crisis will share details. Realizing the flaw in the church's check-in and checkout system, Joan updated their procedures to guard against anyone—even a family member—picking up a child without permission. She trained her team using her own situation as a case study.

Joan's story has an even happier ending. A few months later, she received a card in the mail. One of the children had crafted a personalized note on card stock. Joan could feel a knot forming in her throat as she read the words written in colorful marker: "Ms. Joan, thank you for being my teacher. I love your Bible lessons. This week I accepted Jesus into my heart. I want you to baptize me."

6

# PROTECTING AND EQUIPPING STUDENTS

Everyone was having a great time on the lake trip. Cliques were breaking down among the students. Two middle schoolers professed faith in Christ. The new volunteers were beginning to form bonds. And the weather was spectacular. Then Jonathan, the ministry leader, received an angry text: "They aren't wearing life jackets! How could you let this happen?"

One of the parents had seen a post on social media and noticed her daughter on a boat without a life jacket. Jonathan cringed because he knew it was an oversight. He had reminded the students multiple times, but a few had still neglected to put them on. Other text messages soon followed. The parents were looking at social media posts and questioning everything.

"Why do they have their phones? I thought they weren't allowed."

"I don't like some of the swimsuits the girls are wearing."

"Are they wearing sunscreen?"

"Can you tell me if my son is taking his medicine at night?"

Eventually the parents got the answers they needed, and the week proceeded without any additional drama.

Most parents of teenagers feel the urgency of equipping their kids for life in the real world. They hit middle school before we know it, we blink, and then they are young adults and out of the house.

One of the most pressing challenges facing the church in recent years is nothing new. Most pastors and church leaders understand that young adults are prone to leave the church, and many never return. Studies conducted by Rainer Research and LifeWay Research revealed the enormous gravity of the problem: 70 percent of those who drop out of church will do so between the ages of eighteen and twenty-two.[1] But the big turning point is when teens reach the age of sixteen. That's when the problems begin to manifest. From sixteen onward, the churn of dropping out worsens until they reach their early twenties.

It is both terrifying and stirring that we are losing so many young adults within such a short window of their lives. But if the church can become vital again to people in this age group, it will solve most of the dropout problem. The youngest generation is our nation's most diverse and best educated.[2] Enormous potential exists for them to have a positive impact on the world. The first step to retaining students and reaching their friends is keeping them safe.

## Ten Nonnegotiable Rules for Student Safety

Student ministry is often where rules about minors break down in the church. Student ministries don't need *fewer* rules than children's ministries, but they need *different* rules. Though rebellion seems to be a rite of passage for many teenagers, they are far more receptive to guidance than you might think. Young people need leaders to shoot straight with them. About life. With biblical depth. We don't need to wade in the shallows and soft pedal the Christian faith. Instead, we must shepherd our youth through the depths of Scripture and the valleys of life. Be clear and honest with them.

One sure way to confuse the younger generation is to set expectations and then not hold anyone accountable. A lack of transparency from adults is frustrating to teenagers. The younger generation tends to follow leaders who are transparent rather than distant or detached. And they want to know they're not alone in their struggles.

You should also realize that many teens carry a burden of guilt, often with no concept of true forgiveness. They need to hear leaders tell them plainly what the atonement of Christ means. They need to hear how the debt of sin has been canceled and how Jesus can save them. Church safety is a core gospel issue. Teenagers will struggle to grasp the Good News if the church delivering the message is unsafe. Consider the following best practices for building better student safety systems in our churches.

### 1. *"Never alone" applies to teens as well*

As in children's ministry, leaders, staff members, and volunteers should always have a third party present when meeting with a student. This rule applies to vehicle rides as well. If a situation requires one-on-one counseling, meet in a room with a camera, leave the door slightly ajar, and make sure another responsible adult is nearby. There may be times when you end up alone with a student unintentionally. For example, parents might be late picking up their teen and you're the only one available to stay until they arrive. In such an instance, contact the parents and let them know the situation. If the parents are unavailable, contact another church leader. Maintain a safe social distance from the student until the parents arrive.

### 2. *Report any reasonable suspicion of abuse*

Take all accusations seriously. The process for reporting abuse with teens is the same as with children. Do not delay, and do not conduct an internal investigation before calling the proper authorities. As mentioned in the previous chapter, each state has different guidelines on mandatory reporting. It is good to know these guidelines, but every adult leader in the student ministry must take personal responsibility for reporting any known or suspected abuse.

### 3. Document all major problems and incidents

I hope you won't have to deal with biting incidents or uncontrolled tantrums in your student ministry, as you might with younger children. But you should document any instances of bullying, injuries that occur on the church campus, and dangerous behavior exhibited by students. Parents and guardians of the students involved should receive a copy of these reports, and leaders in the student ministry should use these situations to take corrective measures.

### 4. Offer professional counseling to those who can't afford it

Unfortunately, you may encounter problems among young people that require professional guidance. Every church should have a benevolence fund to get people started with a counselor. Even if you are able to pay for only a couple of sessions, this gesture will go a long way toward demonstrating a high level of care for individuals experiencing abuse or trauma.

### 5. Never promise confidentiality

If a student approaches you and asks for your help but doesn't want anyone else to know, you should never promise confidentiality. You should also quickly correct other adults who tell students they are "a safe place" and will not share their secrets with others. Such behavior is inappropriate and could possibly indicate that someone doesn't have the young person's best interests in mind. Many states have legal prohibitions against this kind of confidentiality. More critically, secrecy is often how spiritual abuse—and other types of abuse—begins.

### 6. Avoid excessive off-hours time with students

Unhealthy relationships can form when an adult spends too much time with students outside of normal ministry. These bonds can begin innocently but grow quickly due to the emotional attachments young people make. Some teens will request extra time with you. While occasionally hanging out with a group of teens is usually harmless, be cautious of the amount of time you spend with any one individual, even if it's in group settings. Be doubly aware of any tendency on your part or the student's to overly focus on your personal relationship.

### 7. Provide clear, written leadership accountability guidelines

A one-page checklist is an excellent way to remind volunteers of their responsibilities in student ministry. If you're the leader, create a bullet-point checklist for all leaders to have in their possession. Use ongoing training sessions to review the checklist and remind everyone of the accountability systems in place. When these guidelines are violated, deal with the responsible person immediately.

### 8. Limit texting and social media interaction with students

In many cases, students will need your cell-phone number. There are also good reasons why you may be connected on social media. But remember, you are in their lives to equip them spiritually, not to be the cool friend they send silly messages to late at night. Be the adult in your relationships with students. Even when you are connected digitally, maintain a proper rapport. Here is a good rule of thumb: Any message you send to a student should be appropriate for anyone else in the church to view. When you type a message, imagine your words projected on the screen in a worship service for all to see.

### 9. Zero tolerance for pornography

Unfortunately, pornography is ubiquitous, easily accessible, and largely tolerated by our culture. If I could pick one thing to eradicate from this planet, it would be pornography. Thirty years ago, when I was coming of age, pornography was limited in supply and difficult for a young teenager to obtain. Today, all it takes is a little curiosity and an online search to plaster the screen full of inappropriate images. Why is porn so harmful, especially to young people? In the brain of an adolescent, the area that governs emotions develops faster than the impulse control center—which may help to explain why teenagers lack the maturity to control the sexual desires and behaviors roused by pornography.[3]

When you encounter a teen viewing pornography, you should inform the parents and document the activity in an incident report if it occurred on the church campus or at a church-sanctioned event. Of particular concern are the cases of teens sending each other sexually explicit images of themselves. In many states, "sexting" is illegal for anyone under eighteen, and the images could be considered child pornography, even if sent between two consenting minors.[4] Any possession of such images by anyone—underage minor or adult—should be reported to the proper authorities. Additionally, the church should seek legal counsel to understand the best next steps.[5]

### 10. Use the six-month rule for potential volunteers

You should implement a six-month waiting period for anyone wanting to serve in areas of the church with minors. As mentioned in the previous chapter, people who intend to harm will seek out organizations and churches with lax standards, especially churches desperate for volunteers. No amount of desperation should cause a church to sacrifice safety.

## More Exposed, Less Equipped

Students are more exposed to potential harm than ever before, and they are less equipped than ever to deal with this exposure. Anxiety tops the list of problems that teens identify among their peers, even more than bullying or addiction.[6] Tens of millions of Gen Z teens share their locations with their parents via cell phone because they fear what might happen while they're driving, on a date, at a party, or in a large gathering, such as a concert.[7] Where previous generations relished the opportunity for freedom when they were teenagers, anxiety causes Gen Z to desire more connection to their parents. The church should be a place of safety for young people to learn how to cope with the inevitable difficulties of life. I fear that some parents try to remove too much stress for their teens, while other young people have a heavy burden no one should ever carry alone.

The core of anxiety is the fear of losing what you love or getting what you hate. What do teens most fear losing? Freedom? Control? Family? Some people become anxious about losing material items such as jewelry or a vehicle. Nobody wants to lose what they love, but people who struggle with anxiety have a heightened level of fear.

Anxiety also surfaces through the unreasonable fear of getting what you hate. For example, some young people obsess about getting a disease or being shunned by a social group.

Feeling pressure, being broken, or having concerns about losing something important is not sinful. But how can we know when our *concerns* have crossed into the territory of *anxiety*? When we stop placing our trust in God.

Anxiety amplifies our mistrust of God. In the apostle Peter's first letter, he reminds the church, "Give all your worries and cares to God, for he cares about you."[8] The basis of casting our anxieties on God is that he cares for us. We demonstrate one of two things when we don't give him our concerns: We either believe he doesn't care for us, or we believe he isn't powerful enough to handle our concerns. Both are lies from Satan. A regular appearance of anxiety eventually degrades our belief in God's sovereignty. If God is in complete control, and we believe it, then there is never a reason to worry.

Consider Proverbs 12:25: "Worry weighs a person down; an encouraging word cheers a person up." I don't want to oversimplify the problem. For many people, anxiety is a legitimate medical issue. But much of our anxiety doesn't rise to that level. Do you know what might change a person's world? A kind word. Yes, it's that simple. The above proverb reminds us of the power of an encouraging word. As much as the world may push somebody down, we can pull them up by a mere act of kindness.

Satan wants to weigh us down to a place without hope. And teens can be especially susceptible. But the hope of Jesus conquers defeatism, anxiety, fear, doubt, and even death. Our worries have an answer.

We can experience calm in the midst of the storm. God provides assurance even when we aren't sure. And victory is guaranteed because Jesus is alive. Jesus is more powerful than our darkest days. The students in your church need to hear this message repeated time and time again. Encouragement is one of the greatest equipping tools we have as Christians, and church leaders and members should use it more often. Walk with your students in the valley and point them upward to the mountaintop.

7

# HEALING AFTER A CHURCH LEADER FAILS

"Pastor Wes, I need you to come back to the office *right now.*"

The fact that Dave, the chair of the church's personnel committee, would call him in the middle of the day told Wes that something serious was happening. The tone of Dave's voice confirmed it.

"I'll be right there."

Wes pushed his lunch plate away, apologized to his wife and kids for having to leave so suddenly, and strode briskly out to the car.

When Wes arrived at the church, Dave was clearly upset.

"I had no idea. Everything blew up this morning. You need to tell us what to do."

The church's beloved worship pastor, Mark, had been caught in a moral failure. Rumors had been circulating for weeks among the choir members. They had observed how Mark interacted with one of the altos—a married woman with three children. Wes had addressed the situation when the rumors first began, but Mark had calmly and confidently denied everything. Yes, he had enjoyed a conversation or two with Sarah after practice, but it was nothing out of the ordinary.

Because Mark handled the rumors so graciously, Wes concluded that the other choir members were making a mountain out of a molehill. But now Dave had discovered that the rumors were true.

"How did you find out?" Wes asked Dave.

"Sarah's husband, Justin, became suspicious and checked her Facebook messages and texts this morning. He discovered that Sarah and Mark were planning to run away together. They had a date set—three weeks from now. Plane tickets were purchased. She was going to leave Justin and the kids for Mark. Justin went over to Mark's house to confront him, but Mark wasn't there. That's when he called me."

"Do we know where Mark is?"

Dave looked down at his shoes. "He's in the conference room."

Wes sighed, gathered his thoughts, and went to talk to Mark. Was he repentant? Was there remorse? It wasn't easy to tell. Mark mumbled his responses and had trouble putting his thoughts into words. Wes laid out the path forward.

Mark would resign immediately. Wes would read a statement to the church the following Sunday. He would not reveal any details, but the congregation would know that an undisputed moral failure had occurred and that Mark was disqualified from ministry.

As Wes left the room, he wondered whether the planned getaway was still on. He went back to his office and called Justin.

## A Major Problem: No Consensus

Few models exist for how to handle a church leader's moral failure. Indeed, there is little consensus among pastors about what to do, even with something as egregious and explicit as adultery. When researchers asked a group of one thousand pastors, "If a pastor commits adultery, how long, if at all, should the pastor withdraw from public ministry?" almost one-third of the respondents—and remember, these were *pastors*, not just church members—were "not sure." One in five believed the pastor should step down for one year or less, while 27 percent believed the pastor should withdraw permanently from public ministry.[1]

If a pastor is dealing with the moral failure of a staff person and calls peers for advice, the likelihood is high that those peers will give widely different answers. How can a pastor have discernment in such a situation? How can a congregation know what to do? The next section provides some filters to help with a path forward.

## Five Levels of Moral Failure

Crises in ministry are inevitable. Unforeseen events happen. I'll never forget the time our church building was struck by lightning *twice* in the same month. Our insurance agent didn't question the claims, but he did say he wondered about our faithfulness to God. (I'm almost certain he was kidding.)

Understanding the severity of the crisis is important. When a church employee uses an expletive while talking with a member, a conversation with leadership about controlling the tongue is warranted. But this kind of mistake is much less severe than other moral failures.

If the fire department has an emergency dispatch system to determine the proper level of response to a 911 call, and if the National Weather Service uses the Enhanced Fujita Scale to assess the damage level of a tornado, then church leaders should have a way to discern the severity and potential damage of a moral failure. All moral failures are sin, but not every failure has the same consequences. Moral failures can be complex, but the following five levels will help you discern the potential damage and calibrate your response.[2]

### Level 1: When the failure affects only the person involved

People can fail themselves without necessarily affecting other people. Sin almost always involves more than the sinner, but there are times its impact on others is limited. The sin of gluttony, for example. It can affect others, but the greater concern is for the person's health. Level 1 failures should not be ignored, but the effect of this failure on other people is likely to be minimal.

*Level 2: When the failure affects a few people, with little lasting impact*

A level 2 failure will affect a few people, but the potential for lasting damage is small. An example of a level 2 failure would be the abuse of a church credit card. Assume you have a student pastor who uses the church's credit card to buy daily lunches at a local sandwich shop. He explains it away as a time to disciple students. The finance committee has asked him to stop using his budget for these almost daily meal purchases, but he persists. In this case, the finance committee may start to question the student pastor's character, but the meal purchases are unlikely to bring lasting damage to the church.

*Level 3: When the failure has the potential for a lasting impact*

A church was facing a severe cash crunch. The problem was that only a few people in the church knew about the deterioration of the church's finances. The senior pastor refused to tell anyone beyond his small, loyal circle. This pastor was well-loved in the congregation, but his failure to divulge the financial condition of the church had the potential to create lasting problems. The pastor did not maliciously lead the church toward financial instability, so his failure would not likely hurt anyone personally. However, his lack of disclosure could hurt the church in the longer-term. If only he had told people what was happening, they likely would have stepped up and given money to help solve the problem. His failure to inform the church was a violation of trust.

### Level 4: When the failure has a lasting impact and will hurt many people

A lead pastor regularly uses inappropriate words to intimidate people who disagree with him. A preschool director utilizes unapproved, forceful disciplinary measures on children without their parents' knowledge. A worship pastor has a caustic leadership style and throws loud tantrums in the choir room when people don't perform to his standards. A student pastor encourages the bullying of some less popular students on social media. These actions may not hurt everyone in the church, but they will hurt many people. Additionally, the potential damage to the church's reputation could last for a long time.

### Level 5: When the failure has a permanent impact on the entire church

This kind of failure can permanently destroy a church. When a pastor or staff person commits adultery, abuses a child, embezzles money from the church, or is convicted of a felony and goes to jail, it is clearly a level 5 moral failure. The fallout affects the entire church and can permanently damage its reputation in the community.

Pastors don't fall into extreme moral failure overnight. It's often the result of a series of poor choices leading up to the crowning instance of failure. They choose isolation over community. They stop confessing their sins. Then they start to sin without any consideration of the consequences. Why would a church leader not consider the fallout of potential bad behavior? Morally compromised pastors start to believe the rules no longer apply to them. They think their position and power allow them to make their own choices without accountability.[3] Whether you are a pastor or a congregant, I hope you never experience the pain of this level of failure. Unfortunately, some pastors and churches will suffer from some degree of moral failure. What steps can you and your church take to heal after it happens?

## The Path Forward After a Moral Failure

How should you devise a plan of action following a pastor or staff member's moral failure? Obviously, you would address the issue of gluttony differently than you would adultery. The following questions will help you determine a way forward after a leader's moral failure.

### 1. What is the degree of offense?

Use the five levels of moral failures as a filter to determine the magnitude of the offense. These levels will not encompass every type of moral failure, but they are useful for understanding the degree of offense. Avoid making quick decisions if possible. When leaders make emotional decisions, the repercussions are often not good. Take the necessary time to understand the entire situation. Too many leaders make the mistake of finalizing decisions without hearing from all the involved parties. When analyzing the situation, no leader should act alone. When moral failure occurs on a church staff, leaders need the advice of trusted counselors inside and outside the church.

*2. Is the staff member accepting or denying responsibility?*

Allegations of a moral failure are much different than an admission of a moral failure. If the pastor or staff member denies the accusations, the path forward must include an investigation. Most pastors (73 percent) believe allegations should be kept in confidence with church leaders during an investigation.[4] If the allegations include crimes, let the proper authorities conduct the investigation rather than performing one internally. For allegations that are not criminal in nature, you should meet with both the accuser and the accused—separately at first—and you should have a trusted third party in the meeting as a witness. Of course, there may be cases in which bringing together the accuser and the accused would be unwise. Bring in the elders, the personnel committee, or whatever group helps to oversee the staff. If no such group exists, bring in a couple of other trusted church leaders.

*3. What is the level of remorse?*

If the person admits to the moral failure, you should discern their level of remorse. When someone is ready to repent, the process should include much grace. When the person is defiant, the process should include firm discipline.

### 4. What are the church's policies and covenants?

Many churches have clear guidelines detailing the process of working through a moral failure. Many churches also have a covenant for pastors and staff that provides biblical support for the process of discipline or reconciliation. Before you move forward with a plan, make sure you understand the guidelines in the church's policies, as well as any covenantal requirements governing the person in question.

## Why Some Churches Tolerate Bad Behavior

Most pastors work hard, love their churches, and sacrifice their lives for the people they serve. But there are bad pastors out there. Why do people stay with them? What makes followers susceptible to toxic leadership? There are three main reasons this breakdown happens.

*A desire for safety.* Most of us are not locked in to a particular leader. We can vote with our feet and leave a church. We can look for a new job. We can transfer schools. We can vote out politicians and strike against companies. Most followers in our culture have the freedom to walk away. But with every increase in freedom comes a corresponding decrease in safety. If we walk away from a job, the corresponding paycheck is no longer guaranteed. If we vote out a politician, we risk voting for someone worse. In short, some followers stick with bad leaders because they are unwilling to risk their safety in the hopes of finding greater freedom. Leaving a church can be a complex process, especially when you've been there for a long time or have children who feel safe in their surroundings. Some people stay in toxic congregations because they believe that sticking with the familiar—even if it's unhealthy—is better than venturing into the unknown.

*A desire for belonging.* Ditching a bad leader may mean leaving a long-standing community. Loyalty is a powerful force within an established group. Belonging to a human community will often supersede leaving a bad group leader.[5] It's why some churchgoers tolerate a fruitless pastor. It's why many cult followers do not denounce the cult even after the leader falters catastrophically. Unfollowing a toxic leader is often more painful because of the sense of belonging that comes from the community over which the leader presides.

*A desire for comfort.* Challenging bad leaders is uncomfortable (at best) and deadly (at worst), but many followers forget they can challenge their leaders. In fact, dual accountability is one of the keys to a successful leader-follower relationship. To challenge leaders, however, followers must let go of comfortable silence. If you are the only one to speak out, and no one joins you, you're left alone in a vulnerable position. Many followers are not willing to risk comfort to challenge bad leaders.

Accountability is part of what prevents pastors from becoming dictators and tyrants. Congregants need shepherds to help guide them to better places. Pastors need church members to fulfill God's purpose for the church. This dual accountability is the glue sticking followers with leaders (or congregants and pastors).

## Leading Your Church to Heal

When a church leader has a moral failure, you must have a plan not only for the guilty individual but also for the church. Both the leader and the congregation need a path forward toward healing. First and foremost, you must tell the truth. The church should know about the moral failure. It is impossible to heal unless you know what has hurt you. There is no need to share all the details or the other parties involved, but the church should understand the big picture of what happened. If you're the lead pastor, you should teach about healing from sin. Put the current sermon series on hold and focus on working through the current situation. Also, it is important to spend time with people, especially those most affected and most in pain.

### Terminate (when necessary) with grace and compassion

When a leader's moral failure brings significant pain to a congregation, the most likely outcome is termination. But this severing of the relationship must occur with a high level of compassion. The church may choose to provide for the leader's family for a season. When a pastor's sins are to the degree of disqualification from ministry, the decision to pay severance can be more complicated. Some will call for justice and want to cut off the pastor immediately. Others will want to extend grace and help the family for a time of transition. Every case has its own particulars. And while it's difficult to prescribe a general rule for disqualified pastors, I believe the best path is to offer a one- to three-month severance to help the family. They are suffering the consequences of the leader's fall in ways the congregation can only imagine. Rarely will a church regret having adopted a posture of grace and generosity, even in the most difficult situations.

### Assist with reconciliation and counseling

Even if a pastor is terminated for adultery, the church should still pursue God's ideal for marriage. Perhaps the church can be a catalyst for reconciliation between the spouses. Though a pastor may be disqualified from ministry, the church should help to restore the marriage. Additionally, the church should provide assistance to those hurt by the pastor's actions by paying for counseling services to aid in the healing process.

### Encourage everyone to pray

Do not overlook the spiritual power of prayer. When a church suffers through the moral failure of a leader, everyone in the congregation should pray. The temptation will be to follow human wisdom. Prayer prompts the church to seek God's wisdom.

The pain will last for a while, and at times it may seem intolerable. Even church leaders may be tempted to move to another church just to escape the situation. But leading your church toward healing is of paramount importance. Churches facing this type of pain need their pastors to take ownership of the situation and model the grace and mercy of Christ. And one day, Jesus will resolve all the pain.

# TAKING RESPONSIBILITY
# FOR CHURCH SAFETY

"I'll do it," one of the deacons said as he raised his hand. "I can make sure these kids have a safe way to get to church and back home."

A group of elementary students who lived in a tough neighborhood needed transportation in order to attend church on Sundays. They had first come to the church for Vacation Bible School and loved it. Their parents weren't interested in attending church, but they said their kids could go if someone gave them a ride. The deacons were now discussing the situation at their monthly meeting.

"I can use the church van and create the pickup and

drop-off schedule each week," said the first deacon. "But I need someone to ride with me to fulfill our safety requirements."

"I can ride," another deacon said, raising his hand as if he were still in school.

"Me too." Another hand went up on the other side of the table.

"Thank you," the pastor said with a smile. "I believe we can reach the entire neighborhood, and this ministry could be the start of something incredible."

Discipleship occurs within the community of the church; it's not possible to be a solo disciple. Accountability is impossible apart from a body of believers. As the apostle Paul writes to the Romans, "We are many parts of one body, and we all belong to each other."[1] No one can accomplish God's mission alone. The foot, apart from the leg, can't walk. The hand, apart from the arm, can't embrace. The local church is an expression of the body of Christ. We are his hands and feet, doing his work on earth. Jesus is the head, guiding and directing us in this work.

The process of making disciples involves the entire church working together. Still, church safety won't happen the way it should until every person in a ministry decides to make it an individual priority. Safe churches develop when people are individually committed to protecting the vulnerable. Safety is not someone else's responsibility. Safety is not *everyone's* responsibility. A safe church is one where the people are willing to say, "Safety is *my* responsibility."

How do you begin? Consider the familiar passage in James 1:26-27:

> If you claim to be religious but don't control your
> tongue, you are fooling yourself, and your religion
> is worthless. Pure and genuine religion in the sight
> of God the Father means caring for orphans and
> widows in their distress and refusing to let the world
> corrupt you.

Much can be learned from these two pithy verses. James is specific and to the point: *Do* what you believe. Your internal purity will drive your external responsibility. In short, holiness always takes action. You don't want to fool yourself with worthless religion. Pure and genuine believers will not be corrupted by the world, and this internal purity will lead them to care for and protect the vulnerable.

*Do what you hear* was a common message among the Old Testament prophets.[2] What we do doesn't save us, but it does validate what we say we believe. The way we know we are faithful to God's Word is that we look after others who are less fortunate. But we also know we are true to God's Word when we refuse to be polluted by the world.

Some churches upset the balance between internal purity and external responsibility. Some will fight for justice and stand up for the oppressed, but then they accept people regardless of moral purity. "We don't want to judge," they say.

Other churches fight for "family values" and holiness, but

they don't do much to help those who are hurting. "People need to straighten up and fly right" seems to be their primary message.

The Bible teaches that both internal purity and external responsibility are required of Christ's followers. On a personal level, we can't divide our lives. It's impossible to separate our personal devotion from our everyday actions. The time we spend with God doesn't occur in a vacuum. We will not live holy lives if we are not regularly in God's Word. Conversely, our actions will drag us away from God's Word if we are not living holy lives. Personal holiness leads to a lifestyle that puts others first. And when we commit to living selflessly, we more clearly reflect the righteousness of Christ.

What if your legacy was that nobody remembered your name, but everyone you encountered remembered Jesus because of how you lived your life?

More than fifty years ago, Joe Hendrickson, a high school football coach, decided he would share the gospel with all his players no matter the cost. Practice after practice, year after year, he pulled out his Bible and explained to his team that no one deserves salvation, just death. He then told his team that Christ took the punishment for our sin and explained how Jesus saves.

My father happened to be on one of Coach Hendrickson's teams. He accepted Christ because the coach was willing to live out his faith consistently.

A few years ago, my father wrote a new Bible study curriculum, and guess who happened to read it at church? His old coach. Coach Hendrickson called the publisher's customer service line and told the representative his story. Not long after—but more than forty years after my father graduated from high school—Coach Hendrickson and my dad got together, and they talked about the gospel. As Christians, we cannot separate who we are from what we do. The foundation of church safety is rooted in our commitment to both personal holiness and individual responsibility.

## A Personal Covenant for Church Safety

A covenant is a promise we make to God—and often to another person or group of people. The vertical aspect of a covenant describes how we direct this promise to God. The horizontal aspect is how we direct the same promise to others. Marriage is a great example. Today, many view marriage as a way to find emotional and relational fulfillment, but marriage is not a private arrangement meant to satisfy two individuals. Marriage is a public covenant for God's greater good.

The "What's in it for me" view of marriage places a crushing burden on both spouses, because they cannot fulfill God's place in the other's life.

On the other hand, the "What can I do in service to God" view of marriage is a freeing sacrifice through which we give first and receive second. Marriage is not based on self-fulfillment but on self-denial. The covenant view of marriage means a common horizon exists for both husband and wife, both looking toward the throne of God. We help each other get to "Well done, good and faithful servant." The true bond of marriage is our commitment to our spouse's holiness.

In the same way, the church should be committed to the holiness of each individual within the body. An unsafe church becomes a pollutant to holiness. When we make a personal commitment to church safety, we are in effect making a covenant with God and others that we will do everything in our power to protect the vulnerable. What might this covenant look like? Below is an example you can use.[3]

> I [NAME] commit to minister in ways that assure the safety and spiritual growth of all our children, youth/students, and vulnerable people. I will make my church safe by reporting any suspicions of neglect or abuse. I will complete all required safety training and submit to regular reference checks required by the church. I will follow policies, procedures, and guidelines set by my church. I promise to do everything in my power to make my church safe.

Taking personal responsibility means recognizing and accepting the role you play in achieving the desired outcome, understanding the implications of your actions, and being accountable for the results. A covenant is a good starting point for helping your church achieve the goal of having a culture of safety. But for longstanding cultural change to occur, you will need more than a covenant.

## Moving Safety beyond Policies and into Church Culture

If you pastor a church of any size, you must manage the organization—which involves a combination of *technical* and *cultural* issues. Technical matters—such as facilities management, curriculum selection, and program coordination—require specific expertise, but often they can be handled by a single leader or a committee. Cultural issues, on the other hand, are pervasive to the organization and cannot be solved by technical expertise. Instead, these issues involve general acceptance by everyone. There's a reason why certain things become embedded in the culture of a church; usually it's because most people find them acceptable. Having people sign a covenant is a good step toward establishing common values, but the action itself is merely technical. To bring about true change, those values must be internalized. Likewise, holding volunteers accountable to safety policies and procedures is necessary, but if people don't take ownership of the process, you may not achieve the culture you desire.

Consider the following insight from former business consultant Ron Ashkenas:

All change in organizations is challenging, but perhaps the most daunting is changing culture. There are at least two reasons for this: (1) Culture is a soft concept. If there's no concrete way of defining or measuring culture, then how can you change it? And (2) culture represents collective norms and behaviors. It's hard enough to change one person's behavior—how can you change the behavior of an entire organization?[4]

Indeed, changing the behavior of an entire congregation is a significant endeavor. How can you ensure that safety becomes embedded in the culture of your church? Here are six simple guidelines.

*The message must be clear.* What the leaders communicate about safety must be cohesive, consistent, and continual. When different ministries within the same church have different standards, it causes confusion. Culture doesn't change for the better when people lack clarity. Most churches experience a 30 percent turnover of the congregation each year—which means you lose an average of one-third of your people while gaining about the same number.[5] Because of this ongoing cycle, you must communicate about safety repeatedly throughout the year. Regular communication of a consistent and cohesive message is necessary to change the culture in your church.

*Expectations must be high.* God's mission on earth requires an all-in, all-out effort from everyone in the congregation. Churches with high expectations tend to assimilate people better, as more demanding environments equate to greater allegiance and greater meaning.[6] Can a church become too intense with its requirements? Of course, but such churches are rare in North American culture. Far more churches should have higher expectations of their members than they do. A low-expectation environment creates a lax culture in which safety is compromised.

*Training must be repeated often.* Culture shifts in the right direction when we reinforce our expectations through regular training. Most church volunteers want to know what to do, and they have no problem following the rules as long as they have been equipped. Ongoing training empowers people to act. When they are well-versed in the safety guidelines, they can quickly identify and respond to unsafe situations. Without regular training, people are less likely to take action to address an unsafe environment—not out of fear but because of unawareness.

*Discipline must be fair.* When someone intentionally doesn't follow the guidelines in a ministry, there must be consequences. Be reasonable in your discipline. The consequences should be different for someone who leaves an outside door propped open to let in air than for a leader or volunteer who drives a teenager home without another adult in the vehicle. When the guidelines are not fairly and uniformly enforced, it sends a message that any behavior is acceptable. A negative culture forms when discipline is absent or unfair.

*Exceptions must be rare.* Is there ever a time when an exception to the rules should be allowed? Yes, but these should be few and far between. It's impossible to foolproof your policies and procedures for every possible occurrence, so there must be some room for a leader to exercise good judgment. But again, those exceptions should be rare. I once saw a child get injured, and I stayed with the child alone while another person went to get help. In a positive church culture, almost everyone will recognize when an exception is appropriate. But when exceptions become the rule, it communicates that the guidelines are merely suggestions.

*Celebrations must be big.* Whatever a church routinely celebrates will inevitably become rooted in the culture of the congregation.

I'll never forget the words of a woman in her seventies who came to Christ because her grandson invited her to his baptism at our church.

"The service was good, and the baptism was quick," she later told me, "but what I experienced at the party changed me."

She had become open to hearing the gospel when she saw how the entire church celebrated with her grandson after the service.

"It was when they brought out the birthday cake to signify his new birth that I began to cry," she said. "When the church began to sing, I realized I had never experienced such joy, and I knew that I wanted to have this joy."

What you celebrate becomes a leading indicator of what you believe is important. Celebrations help to form the culture. Observe what a congregation celebrates, and you will gain insight into the culture of that church.

Church safety is your responsibility. A safe church culture will never form until a significant number of people make a personal commitment to it. My father is a Christian because a high school coach decided that God's Kingdom was more important than anything else—even football. My parents raised me in the faith, so perhaps it could be said that I, too, am a believer in Jesus because of Coach Hendrickson. Your commitment to church safety will affect the culture of your church and foster an environment in which discipleship can thrive. And it may also make an eternal difference in someone's life.

9

# THE KINGDOM STRENGTH
# OF A SAFE CHURCH

As we've now seen, every church has a dual calling of safety and danger, and every church member is responsible for making their church *internally* safe so they can be *externally* dangerous to evil. When churches are safe inside, people are better equipped to face danger on the outside. An unsafe church works against the mission of God's Kingdom. A safe church is battle-ready to combat the world's problems. When the church body is unsafe, it is unfit for battle. Safe churches make the Kingdom of God a priority. Indeed, you cannot be an effective church in God's Kingdom unless you are a safe place for the vulnerable.

For example, consider what Jesus says about the innocence

and vulnerability of children: "The Kingdom of God belongs to those who are like these children."[1] Moreover, he said, "Anyone who doesn't receive the Kingdom of God like a child will never enter it."[2] The Lord's lesson here is vital. Some parents had brought children to Jesus so he could bless them and heal them, but the culture didn't place a high value on children. Even the disciples were annoyed that some kids were interrupting Jesus' teaching. At the time, children were viewed as the lowest part of society. Often, they would be abandoned. Abuse was tolerated. Many children ended up as slaves because their parents simply did not care for them. It's in this setting that Jesus teaches that children *are* the blessing. The Lord gave value to those who were viewed as least valuable. Kingdom strength comes from protecting the vulnerable. A safe church is a strong church. Safe churches have the courage to care for the vulnerable, the strength to carry the weak, and the passion to share the Good News of Jesus with everyone.

## The Courage to Care

Many younger people are inspired by thoughts of solving the world's injustices. They want to help people who are poor, feed the hungry, elevate the outcast, and free the enslaved. As you grow older, though, time hardens your perspectives. You begin to understand the fruitlessness of naive ideals. The been-there-done-that mentality sinks in and a new viewpoint surfaces: *People get what they deserve.* That's true, but only in part.

I teach my kids that one mark of being a Rainer is that they will learn to work hard for what they get. If I'm a successful parent, my children will not have a sense of entitlement and they will not whine to get their way. But as much as I want to challenge my children, I also want to be gracious and loving toward them.

In the church we face the same balancing act. How can we be both *strong* and *soft*? *Courageous* and *caring*? *Safe* for people and *dangerous* to evil?

Courage is the ability to do what is right in the face of fear and danger. It's the willingness to do what is unpleasant—to sacrifice yourself for others and stand for the truth, whatever the cost. There are many examples of courage in the Bible, but consider Mary, the mother of Jesus.

In Luke 1, an angel visits Mary and shares how the miraculous will happen through her. She will conceive the Savior of the world by the Holy Spirit.

How does Mary respond to the angel? "I am the Lord's servant," she says. "May everything you have said about me come true."[3] Her courage was rooted in God's sovereignty. We can do what is right because *he* is right. We can face fear because *he* has defeated the powers of darkness. We are able to sacrifice because Christ has already offered the perfect sacrifice.

There is a quick, obscure reference to Mary in Luke 11. While Jesus is teaching, a woman in the crowd interrupts him and says, "Your mom is awesome!"[4] More specifically, she says that Mary's womb is blessed.

Jesus replies that Mary is blessed not because of her womb

but because she obeys God's Word. The blessing is for those who "hear the word of God and put it into practice."[5] Mary is a model of courage but Jesus ranks obedience to God's Word above any blessing.

God gives courage, and we find courage when we *hear* and *keep* his Word. Godly courage is not risk-taking for personal gain. Godly courage occurs through obedience so that others can gain. You will be afraid at times. Fear is unavoidable. But the moment you face your fear, you have a choice between self-preservation or seeking God's will. It isn't wrong to feel fear, but it is wrong to allow fear to make decisions for us. Courage makes God's work the priority no matter what the cost.

When children need care, their mothers are often the ones they run to. I'm sure that young Jesus was no exception. I'm sure he ran to Mary when he skinned his knee or bumped an elbow. But Mary's ministry was more than bandages for boo-boos. Remember, the red dragon—Satan—wanted to devour the Christ child.[6] Mary was on the front lines of an intense spiritual battle as she raised Jesus. The dragon initiated a fierce attack, but by the power of the Holy Spirit, Mary successfully defended against this onslaught of darkness.

Since Mary cared for Jesus, we can live for Jesus. Mary was with Jesus throughout his time on earth. She gave birth to him, walked with him during his ministry, and watched him die through the brutality of crucifixion. Like Mary's home, our homes are on the front lines of a spiritual battle. Safe churches support safe homes where future warriors are raised to fight the spiritual forces of evil.

God sent Jesus as a helpless baby. Without a caring mother to raise our Savior, the plan of salvation would be incomplete. For Jesus to be *with us*, he had to be *with Mary*, cared for by a loving mother. It was Mary who cared for him as God prepared Jesus for the mission of saving humanity.

Mary experienced excruciating pain at the foot of the cross, but that isn't the last time we see her in the Bible. She appears once more in Acts 1, when she gathers with the apostles in the upper room to pray. We don't know the time or manner of her death, but we do know she carried her son's message of comfort to a world that was dying to hear it. Mary was one of the first missionaries. She was brave, bold, and completely sold out for the cause of Christ. Mary's courage to care was necessary for the salvation of the world. Jesus needed a safe home environment to grow in stature and wisdom. The internal safety provided by Mary and Joseph in their home was part of God's plan to defeat the world's evil. The church today is no different. We must be internally safe for the vulnerable in order to become externally dangerous to evil. In this way, church safety becomes a gospel issue. If the climate inside the church is bad news for some, then the church cannot properly proclaim the Good News to the world.

## The Strength to Carry

A large crowd had gathered in the home of a wealthy person to hear Jesus teach.[7] The Pharisees and scribes were there, along with members of the elite class from all over the region.

Perhaps some hoped to catch Jesus saying something blasphemous. The house was in Capernaum, on the north side of the Sea of Galilee, where Peter was from. As Jesus was teaching, four friends attempted to bring a paralyzed man on a stretcher into the home. But the people inside the house would not give up their places for the disabled man.

What did these four friends do? They went up to the roof, pulled up some tiles, and lowered their paralyzed friend to a spot right in front of Jesus. Why? Though physical healing might seem to be an obvious motive, I don't think it was the main reason they were there. I believe they came for forgiveness.

These friends risked their reputations. The leaders of society were all there, and they had the power to ruin a person's life. Did that stop the friends? No. Not in the least.

They risked financial consequences. They cut a hole in the roof! They didn't seem worried about money.

They risked embarrassment. Did it matter to them that they were causing a scene in front of the entire community? Nope. These friends valued loyalty over self-preservation.

After they tried to enter the house, they could have said to their disabled friend, "Hey man, we tried. There's just no way to get in there." Their determination shows that their loyalty was greater than their desire for self-preservation. And most important, they had faith in what Jesus could do. They had the strength to carry a friend in need.

Jesus recognized their faith—*all* of it. When he forgave the paralyzed man's sins, the Pharisees started thinking he was a blasphemer. Jesus peered into their hearts and knew their thoughts. He asked them, "Why do you question this in your hearts? Is it easier to say 'Your sins are forgiven,' or 'Stand up and walk'?"[8] Jesus then commanded the man to walk. After all, it's one thing to *say* that someone is forgiven. It's another thing to *prove* you have the power to forgive.

The man jumped up as everyone watched, picked up his mat, and went home praising God. The crowd in the home was awestruck. All five friends had faith, but without the four being willing to carry the disabled man, he never would have made it to Jesus on his own. The dangerous calling of safe churches includes carrying the weak and taking risks, so that everyone has a chance to meet Jesus.

## The Passon to Share

"Passion is the degree of difficulty one will endure to reach a goal," my college pastor said in a sermon many years ago. This idea has stuck with me for more than two decades. It will stay with me for the rest of my life. If we are unwilling to endure hardship for someone or something, we are not passionate about them.

Unfortunately, the North American church, by and large, is not passionate about sharing Jesus. A recent Church Answers poll found that only 1 percent of churches have an ongoing evangelism effort.[9] This finding corroborated a more extensive longitudinal study we've conducted since 1996, in which the lowest church health score across denominations is seen in the category of evangelism. And it's only getting worse. We are seeing the same trend across denominational lines and in nondenominational churches. Church health will not improve until evangelism returns.

A renewed focus on evangelism is one of the best ways to rejuvenate church health. The healthiest churches inwardly are the ones most focused outwardly. Ongoing evangelism is a lead-by-example enterprise. Evangelistic churches have evangelistic pastors and church leaders. Frankly, if you are involved in your church, this change begins with you. Ongoing evangelism can start with only a few people. You don't need buy-in from the entire congregation to start changing the culture. Just a few people working together is enough to alter the course of a church. Your church address is not an accident. Your home address is not an accident. Your work address is not an accident. God has sovereignly placed you where you are. Why? Someone in your life right now needs to hear the Good News.

When we follow Christ, he will take us on a journey filled with twists, turns, potholes, dangers, and incredible views. An easy life produces weak and untested people. The difficult times challenge us, strengthen us, and allow us to become more like Christ.

What is your default attitude? The cynics will always have a reason why something can't happen. The apathetic don't care what happens. But then there are the passionate eternal optimists, the ones who say, "I believe God will *make* something happen." Eternal optimists share the gospel because they believe God will save people. Eternal optimists serve the church because they believe God will bring healthy growth and maturity to the congregation. Eternal optimists worship because they know God is present in their midst. Passionate churches are dangerous to the forces of evil. They live out the gospel truth that Satan is defeated and Christ is victorious. Your victory in Christ is greater than anyone's ability to make you afraid!

## Safe Churches with a Dangerous Calling

In Psalm 91, God offers his shelter, refuge, and protection. While he gives his protection, we know from age and experience that the Kingdom of God requires us to encounter danger. God's protection does not mean you are free from pain. When we give our lives to Christ, he does not respond, "Now that you trust in me, nothing bad will happen." God's protection is not about keeping you free from *pain*. Instead, God's protection is all about keeping you free from *sin*.

I'll never forget meeting Laura Yockey for the first time. She scheduled a meeting and arrived precisely on time at my office.

"I want you to know about my calling to missions," she stated matter-of-factly. "Since you are my pastor, I assume you would want to know."

"That's wonderful," I said, and I explained a few options for her to consider.

"Thank you for the information," she responded. "But

I've already saved my money, started a nonprofit, and bought a one-way plane ticket to Rwanda."

"When do you leave?"

"Next week."

I learned two lessons in this meeting. First, do not underestimate someone when they are obedient to God's calling. Second, Laura is one of the most capable people I've ever pastored. What began with a plane ticket and a calling has transformed her region in Rwanda. Her mission agency now educates children, builds schools, feeds families, and provides vocational training for women.[10] After years on the field, Laura has seen her ministry grow tremendously.

Where I thought I was simply encouraging a young woman to consider a short-term missions trip, God was equipping and sending a warrior missionary to a difficult place.

How many more young people like Laura are in our churches? We will never know unless we create a safe environment for them to grow in their faith. Safe churches are sending churches.

Safe churches have a dangerous calling. Dark places need the light of Christ. The internal safety of a Kingdom church provides strength for people to be equipped as daring gospel ambassadors. The vulnerable need a safe place to run to. At the same time, the strong are called into danger.

"Now go," Jesus commands, "I am sending you out as lambs among wolves."[11]

# Notes

INTRODUCTION: A DUAL CALLING
1. Genesis 4:2; Exodus 3:1; 1 Samuel 16:11; Amos 1:1; Luke 2:8-20.
2. Micah 5:2, 4.
3. John 10:14. See also John 10:1-16.
4. *Looking Out for #1*, by Robert Ringer, originally published in 1977, is one of the bestselling self-help books of all time. Ringer's premise is simple: "Looking out for number one begins with the belief that you have a moral right to take actions aimed at giving you the greatest amount of pleasure and least amount of pain, provided your actions do not violate the rights of others" [Robert Ringer, *Looking Out for #1* (New York: Skyhorse, 2013), ix]. This premise is not only flawed, it's also dangerous. Pursuing only pleasure leads to an ingrown, selfish culture in which sacrifice is minimized and self-absorption is maximized.
5. Jessica De Leon, "Bradenton Is Opioid Overdose Capital of Florida. And Still No One Knows Why," *Bradenton Herald*, December 19, 2016, https://www.bradenton.com/news/local/heroin-epidemic/article121725633.html.
6. Psalm 23:2.
7. Exodus 2:6.
8. Exodus 1:16, 22.
9. Luke 11:20.
10. Luke 11:23.
11. Luke 10:18-19.
12. John 14:30.
13. Ephesians 6:11.

CHAPTER 1: THE REALITY OF THIS DARK WORLD

1. Steve Rabey, "Spiritual Warfare, Supernatural Sales," *Christianity Today*, December 9, 1988, https://www.christianitytoday.com/ct/1988/december-9/books.html.
2. See Ephesians 6:12 in the ESV or NRSV.
3. 1 Peter 5:8.
4. 2 Corinthians 11:14.
5. 1 John 4:1, NASB. What are these spirits? They could be angels or demons, good teachers or false prophets, sound spiritual lessons or deceitful guidance. What is clear in the passage is there are two active forces in this world: good and evil.
6. 1 John 4:6.
7. See Deuteronomy 13:1-3. Miracles in the Old Testament are often referenced as "signs" or "wonders." These signs and wonders can be unexpected divine action or a special manifestation of God's power.
8. Acts 19:19.
9. Warren W. Wiersbe, *The Bumps Are What You Climb On* (Grand Rapids, MI: Baker Books, 2006), 75–76.
10. Genesis 3:15.
11. Jude 1:6.
12. Matthew 2:13-15.
13. Matthew 4:1-11.
14. Matthew 16:21-23.
15. Ezekiel 28:14. This section of Ezekiel is cryptic and notoriously difficult to understand. However, the downfall of pride is quite clear.
16. Ezekiel 28:17.
17. Ephesians 6:10-13.
18. My wife would like you to know that we went to the hospital to make sure the break wasn't serious. When the doctor assured her that her nose *wasn't* broken, my wife insisted on an X-ray. She was right—as always.
19. 1 Peter 2:2-3.
20. Hebrews 5:12–6:1, 3.

CHAPTER 2: MITIGATING THE RISKS OF MINISTRY

1. Basyle J. Tchividjian, "Responding with Excellence to an Allegation of Sexual Abuse within the Church," *Currents in Theology and Mission* 45, no. 3 (July 2018): 41, https://currentsjournal.org/index.php/currents/article/view/134/153.
2. "Church Board Guide to Developing a Risk Management Strategy," Church Law & Tax, 2015, 5.

3. For more context on this scandal, see *The Smartest Guys in the Room* by Bethany McLean and Peter Elkind. There is also a movie by the same name. Fair warning: Like the energy industry at the time, the book and the movie are not exactly clean.
4. This section adapted from Sam Rainer, "Five Essential Accountability Standards for Pastors and Paid Church Staff," *Church Answers* (blog), May 10, 2023, https://churchanswers.com/blog/five-essential-accountability -standards-for-pastors-and-paid-church-staff/.
5. You can view my church's covenant at bylaws.westb.org.
6. These standards are codified in our employee handbook and overseen by the personnel committee of our church.
7. Patrick J. Lyons, "An Earthquake Rattles the Midwest," *New York Times*, April 18, 2008, https://archive.nytimes.com/thelede.blogs.nytimes .com/2008/04/18/an-earthquake-rattles-the-midwest/.
8. Nassim Nicholas Taleb, "The Black Swan: The Impact of the Highly Improbable," *New York Times*, April 22, 2007, https://www.nytimes .com/2007/04/22/books/chapters/0422-1st-tale.html.
9. *Merriam-Webster*, s.v. "force majeure," accessed January 30, 2024, https://www.merriam-webster.com/dictionary/force%20majeure.

CHAPTER 3: THE SYSTEMIC PROBLEM OF ABUSE

1. Matthew 2:16.
2. Physical, emotional, and sexual abuse are each different and will affect people in different ways. The purpose of this chapter is not to give a detailed description of each form of abuse, but rather to establish the truth that systemic abuse is prevalent in our culture at large and in our churches.
3. Rachael Denhollander, *What Is a Girl Worth?* (Carol Stream, IL: Tyndale, 2019).
4. Christa Brown, *This Little Light: Beyond a Baptist Preacher Predator and His Gang* (Cedarburg, WI: Foremost Press, 2009), xi.
5. Wade Mullen, *Something's Not Right: Decoding the Hidden Tactics of Abuse and Freeing Yourself from Its Power* (Carol Stream, IL: Tyndale, 2020), 15.
6. Diane Langberg, *Redeeming Power: Understanding Authority and Abuse in the Church* (Grand Rapids, MI: Brazos Press, 2020), 8.
7. Michael J. Kruger, *Bully Pulpit: Confronting the Problem of Spiritual Abuse in the Church* (Grand Rapids, MI: Zondervan, 2022), 33.
8. "Fast Facts: Preventing Child Abuse & Neglect," Centers for Disease Control and Prevention, last reviewed April 6, 2022, https://www.cdc .gov/violenceprevention/childabuseandneglect/fastfact.html.
9. "Fast Facts: Preventing Intimate Partner Violence," Centers for Disease

Control and Prevention, last reviewed October 11, 2022, https://www.cdc
.gov/violenceprevention/intimatepartnerviolence/fastfact.html.

10. Three large, faith-based insurance companies reported 7,095 insurance
claims of sexual abuse by church employees and church members between
1987 and 2007. These three companies insured approximately 160,000
churches. See, Andrew S. Denney, "Child Sex Abusers in Protestant
Christian Churches: An Offender Typology," *Journal of Qualitative
Criminal Justice and Criminology* 12, no. 1 (January 2, 2023), https://
doi.org/10.21428/88de04a1.000ff84d.

11. "Child Sexual Abuse," Rape, Abuse, and Incest National Network
(RAINN), accessed January 30, 2024, https://www.rainn.org/articles
/child-sexual-abuse.

12. Darby A. Strickland, *Is It Abuse? A Biblical Guide to Identifying Domestic
Abuse and Helping Victims* (Phillipsburg, NJ: P&R Publishing, 2020), 65.

13. Robert Downen, Lise Olsen et al., "Abuse of Faith: A Chronicle
Investigation," *Houston Chronicle*, February 10–June 6, 2019, https://
www.houstonchronicle.com/news/investigations/abuse-of-faith/.

14. Matthew 7:15-16.

15. Luke 22:47-48.

### CHAPTER 4: SECURING YOUR PHYSICAL CAMPUS

1. James P. McGarvey and Michael C. Scully, *4 Pillars of Church Safety and
Security: Critical Ingredients of a Successful Team* (Columbus, OH: Church
Safety Guys, 2022), 59.

2. "About the Campaign," Department of Homeland Security, accessed
September 15, 2023, https://www.dhs.gov/see-something-say-something
/about-campaign.

3. Simon Osamoh, *Securing Church Operations: A Seven-Step Plan for Ministry
and Church Security Leaders* (self-published, 2020), 97–99.

4. Vaughn Baker, *The Church Security Handbook: A Practical Biblical Guide
for Protecting Your Congregation in Uncertain Times* (Kansas City, MO:
Strategos International, 2017), 21.

5. Bobby Ross Jr., "Best Practices for Installing Security Cameras at
Your Church," Church Law & Tax, October 26, 2017, https://www
.churchlawandtax.com/keep-safe/facility-management/best-practices
-for-installing-security-cameras-at-your-church/.

6. Kris Moloney, *Defending the Flock: A Security Guide for Church Safety
Directors* (Belle Plaine, MN: Sheepdog Church Security, 2017), 179.

7. Of the fifty active shooter events identified by the FBI in 2022, only two
occurred at churches. See "Active Shooter Incidents in the United States:

2022," Federal Bureau of Investigation, April 2023, 2, https://www.fbi
.gov/file-repository/active-shooter-incidents-in-the-us-2022-042623
.pdf/view.

8. "Active Shooter: How to Respond," U.S. Department of Homeland
Security, October 2008, 2, https://www.dhs.gov/xlibrary/assets/active
_shooter_booklet.pdf.

9. "Guide for Developing High Quality Emergency Operations Plans for
Houses of Worship," U.S. Department of Homeland Security, June 2013,
28, https://www.dhs.gov/sites/default/files/publications/Developing_EOPs
_for_Houses_of_Worship_FINAL.PDF.

10. "Guide for Developing High-Quality Emergency Operations Plans for
Houses of Worship," 30.

CHAPTER 5: PROTECTING AND EQUIPPING CHILDREN

1. For more information about the ministries of Awana and One More Child,
see https://www.awana.org and https://onemorechild.org.

2. "Church Board Guide to a Child Sexual Abuse Prevention Policy," Church
Law & Tax, 2015, 22.

3. I am indebted to Atul Gawande's book *The Checklist Manifesto* (Picador,
2011). I encourage you to get a copy, read it, and apply the principles to
your ministry area.

4. Sarah McDugal, Jennifer Jill Schwirzer, and Nicole Parker, *Safe Churches:
Responding to Abuse in the Faith Community* (Abide Counseling Press,
2019), 107–111.

5. "Mandatory Reporters of Child Abuse and Neglect," US Department of
Health and Human Services: Administration for Children and Families
Administration on Children, Youth and Families Children's Bureau, July
2019, 4.

6. Pam Whitaker, *One More Child Protection and Mandatory Reporting
Training*, 2022.

CHAPTER 6: PROTECTING AND EQUIPPING STUDENTS

1. Thom S. Rainer and Sam S. Rainer III, *Essential Church?: Reclaiming a
Generation of Dropouts* (Nashville: B&H, 2008), 3.

2. Kim Parker and Ruth Igielnik, "On the Cusp of Adulthood and Facing an
Uncertain Future: What We Know About Gen Z So Far," Pew Research
Center, May 14, 2020, https://www.pewresearch.org/social-trends/2020
/05/14/on-the-cusp-of-adulthood-and-facing-an-uncertain-future-what
-we-know-about-gen-z-so-far-2/.

3. Julie Jargon, "What Porn Does to Teen Brains—and How to Keep It Off

Their Devices," *Wall Street Journal*, July 2, 2022, https://www.wsj
.com/articles/what-porn-does-to-teen-brainsand-how-to-keep-it-off
-their-devices-11656718199.

4. "American Teens Are Sexting More and Sexing Less," *The Economist*,
March 26, 2020, https://www.economist.com/united-states/2020/03
/26/american-teens-are-sexting-more-and-sexing-less.

5. Richard R. Hammar, "Essential Guide to Youth Ministry Safety," Church
Law & Tax, 2017, 17.

6. Juliana Menasce Horowitz and Nikki Graf, "Most U.S. Teens See Anxiety
and Depression as a Major Problem among Their Peers," Pew Research
Center, February 20, 2019, https://www.pewresearch.org/social-trends
/2019/02/20/most-u-s-teens-see-anxiety-and-depression-as-a-major
-problem-among-their-peers/.

7. Julie Jargon, "Teens Want Parents to Track Their Phones and Monitor
Their Every Move," *Wall Street Journal*, October 21, 2023, https://
www.wsj.com/tech/personal-tech/track-my-phone-teens-feel-safer-when
-parents-monitor-7ad437ff.

8. 1 Peter 5:7.

CHAPTER 7: HEALING AFTER A CHURCH LEADER FAILS

1. "Pastors' Views on Moral Failure Survey of American Protestant Pastors,"
LifeWay Research, 2020, 5, http://research.lifeway.com/wp-content
/uploads/2020/08/Pastors-Moral-Failure.pdf.

2. Adapted from "How to Handle a Staff Person's Moral Failure," Deeper
Dive, Church Answers Membership, Issue #14.

3. Carey Nieuwhof, "5 Reasons Pastors Fail Morally (And What to Watch for
in Your Own Life)," *Carey Nieuwhof* (blog), accessed January 30, 2024,
https://careynieuwhof.com/5-reasons-pastors-fail-morally-and-what-to
-watch-for-in-your-own-life/.

4. Bob Smietana, "Survey: Few Pastors Say Adulterous Ministers Should Face
Permanent Ban from Pulpit," LifeWay Research, May 10, 2016, https://
research.lifeway.com/2016/05/10/pastors-say-adulterous-ministers-should
-face-ban/.

5. Jean Lipman-Blumen, "Toxic Leaders and the Fundamental Vulnerability
of Being Alive," in *Follower-Centered Perspectives on Leadership*, eds. Boas
Shamir et al. (Greenwich, CT: Information Age Publishing, 2007), 7.

CHAPTER 8: TAKING RESPONSIBILITY FOR CHURCH SAFETY

1. Romans 12:5.

2. For example, consider Isaiah 1:16-20. Verses 16-17 validate verses 18-20.

Forgiven people do good. When we properly listen to God, we will act in a righteous manner.

3. Some language here is derived from "Abuse Prevention Policy Development Guide," Discipleship Ministries of the United Methodist Church, 2018, 19.
4. Ron Ashkenas, "Let's Talk about Culture Change," *Harvard Business Review*, March 22, 2011, https://hbr.org/2011/03/lets-talk-about-culture-change.
5. Thom S. Rainer, "Why Your Church Has to Replace 32 Percent of Its Attendance to Stay Even Each Year," *Church Answers* (blog), January 23, 2023, https://churchanswers.com/blog/why-your-church-has-to-replace-32-percent-of-its-attendance-to-stay-even-each-year/.
6. This correlation is documented in several studies. See, for example, Dean M. Kelley, *Why Conservative Churches Are Growing* (Macon, GA: Mercer University Press, 1995), and Thom S. Rainer, *High Expectations: The Remarkable Secret for Keeping People in Your Church* (Nashville: B&H, 1999).

CHAPTER 9: THE KINGDOM STRENGTH OF A SAFE CHURCH
1. Luke 18:16.
2. Luke 18:17.
3. Luke 1:38.
4. Luke 11:27, author's paraphrase.
5. Luke 11:28.
6. See Revelation 12:3-4.
7. This story is found in Matthew 9, Luke 5, and Mark 2.
8. Luke 5:22-23.
9. This data is derived from a combination of sources: an internal survey of 1,800 church leaders who are members of Church Answers, social media polls, and a longitudinal study from the Know Your Church tool, a proprietary instrument used to assess church health.
10. You can learn more about Laura and her mission work at LoveAliveInternational.com.
11. Luke 10:3.

# About the Author

**Sam Rainer** serves as president of Church Answers and is a cofounder of Rainer Publishing. He is also lead pastor at West Bradenton Baptist Church in Bradenton, Florida. He writes, teaches, speaks, and consults on a variety of church health issues. Sam cohosts the popular podcasts *Rainer on Leadership* and *Est.church*.

Sam is the author of several books, including *The Church Revitalization Checklist, The Surprising Return of the Neighborhood Church*, and *7 Basics of Belonging*. He has written hundreds of articles for several publications and is a frequent conference speaker on church health issues.

Sam holds a BS in finance and marketing from the University of South Carolina, an MA in missiology from Southern Seminary, and a PhD in leadership studies from Dallas Baptist University. He resides in Bradenton, Florida, with his wife and four children.

# Every church *should* be safe.

# Every church *can* be safe.

Make your church safe with
Safe Church Training from
Church Answers.

MakeMyChurchSafe.com

CP1989